SUPERIOR PRODUCT DEVELOPMENT: MANAGING THE PROCESS FOR INNOVATIVE PRODUCTS

A Product Management Book for Engineering and Business Professionals

Clement C. Wilson
The University of Tennessee, Knoxville

Michael E. Kennedy
The University of Tennessee, Knoxville

Carmen J. Trammell
The University of Tennessee, Knoxville

First published 1996
Blackwell Publishers, the publishing imprint of
Basil Blackwell Inc.
238 Main Street
Cambridge, Massachusetts 02142
USA

Basil Blackwell Ltd.
108 Cowley Road
Oxford OX4 1JF
UK

Library of Congress Cataloging-in-Publication Data

Wilson, Clement Card, 1933-
    Superior product development: managing the process for innovative
products / Clement C. Wilson, Michael E. Kennedy, Carmen J. Trammell.
        p.   cm.
    "A product management book for engineering and business
professionals."
    Includes bibliographical references and index.
    ISBN 1-55786-509-4 (paper : alk. paper)
    1. Product management.   2. Production management.   3. New
products – Marketing.   I. Kennedy, Michael E., 1963 –
    II. Trammell, Carmen J., 1952 –   III. Title.
    HF5415.15.W55   1996
    658.5'75 – dc20   95-7533
                                                                          CIP

ISBN 1-55786-509-4 (pb)

British Library Cataloguing in Publication Data
A CIP catalogue record for this book is available from the British Library.

Typeset by Cornerstone Composition Services.
Printed in the USA on acid-free paper.

FOREWORD

This book can be:

- A text for both graduate and advanced undergraduate courses within engineering schools and graduate courses within business schools;
- A reference or handbook for managers within manufacturing corporations who have broad responsibilities for product development activities;
- A reference or handbook for professionals within a particular facet or function of a product development activity who need to understand and collaborate with other activities within the product development program;
- A reference or handbook for those charged with developing or revising a product development process for their enterprise;
- A training manual or augmentation to training materials for people responsible for in-house education and training;
- A reference or handbook for people who must support or who are impacted by product development activities.

Within manufacturing corporations, product development is central for realizing competitive advantages. It is also the integrating process spanning from the up-front efforts to understand the customers' wants and needs, project competitive offerings, and capture research and technology opportunities to the more downstream activities of manufacturing, distribution sales, and service of products that delight customers.

Concepts such as *enterprise integration* have emerged to emphasize the need for collaboration between the different functions in order to deliver winning products. Many of the companies studied abandoned their functional organizations in favor of creating cross-functional teams that took total responsibility for product delivery. People in product planning who have traditionally had the responsibility to interact with customers and perform marketing research to "get the right product" need to understand the engineering and manufacturing challenges about how to "get the product right." The corporate challenge cuts across both perspectives – "getting the right product right" and "getting the product right."

In order to foster the collaboration necessary to achieve enterprise integration and gain competitive privileges, people in different functions need to understand the challenges and activities that take place within the other functions. Compartmentalization and sequential development processes with hand-offs from one function to the next are no longer competitive.

The Product Development Process Model and associated principles and activities presented in this book provide information about the total product development process, from upstream customer inputs to downstream delivery to customers. This type of cohesive knowledge should be very valuable to anyone: student, manager, practitioner, or trainer. Cross-functional training, knowledge, and collaboration are imperatives for competitive success.

Barry Bebb
Vice President for Product Architecture, Retired
Xerox Corporation

DEDICATIONS

This book is dedicated to the following three IBM engineering managers who had a dramatic effect on my experiences in product development:

Walter Cralle, IBM development engineering manager, taught the importance of a philosophical look at engineering, how to ask the critical questions, how to look for the critical variables, and why it is important to determine how a product fails and what its mode of failure is rather than to simply concentrate on how it works.

Bud Beattie, IBM vice president of engineering, taught the importance of keeping the project schedules intact by asking the "right" technical questions during critical problem phases. His leadership style during technical disasters was such that he never asked, "Who is accountable for this mess?" but always, "How do we solve this problem?" This response inevitably led to a race among the engineers to see who could contribute the most to the problem solution. It was always a privilege to present technical solutions to Bud because he understood and appreciated the contribution. It is regrettable that so much of today's management style seems to be fault finding rather than leadership to significant solutions. Part of that problem is the lack of technical people in the key leadership positions.

Carl Queener, IBM Fellow, taught the importance of setting goals of the highest standard of excellence, often those that were a real "stretch." Over and over, he quoted Thomas J. Watson, Sr.'s statement: "If you set mediocrity as your target, you will always be assured of hitting it dead on." We often set out on paths that we were told would not lead to success. However, in the end, many more accomplishments were made than if we had "played it safe."

C.C.W.

CONTENTS

Contents

4   Customer Future Needs Projection   53

5   Technology Selection and Development   77

6   Final Product Definition and Project Targets   95

7   Product Design and Evaluation   117

8 Marketing and Distribution Preparation 159

9 Manufacturing System Design 169

10 Product Manufacture, Delivery, and Use 203

11 Leading and Organizing Product Development 227

Discussion Questions 241

List of Figures

List of Tables

ACKNOWLEDGMENTS

This book is a direct outgrowth of the eight years of research and development activities within the University of Tennessee Superior Engineering Design Program. The authors wish to express their appreciation for the substantial financial and intellectual support of the Superior Engineering Design Program by Alcoa, Ball Research, Clark Equipment, Hewlett-Packard, IBM, Lexmark, Martin Marietta, Nippondenso, NCR, North American Philips, Northern Telecom, Saturn Corporation, Storage Technology Corporation, Texas Instruments, Toyota, the University of Kentucky Advanced Manufacturing Center, and Westinghouse.

Being appointed to the Martin Marietta professorship at the University of Tennessee enabled Clement Wilson to do on-site case studies of superior development performance. An IBM graduate fellowship enabled Michael Kennedy to pursue MS and PhD degrees, in the course of which he developed the Product Development Guide as part of his dissertation research. An IBM grant, along with assistance from Alcoa and the State of Tennessee, created the Engineering Design Center, which delivers this guide to University of Tennessee students via personal computers. An Alcoa grant enabled Carmen Trammell to create the first software version of the Product Development Model. Grants from the Saturn and Westinghouse corporations enabled the Superior Engineering Design Program to provide actual product development experiences to students in the undergraduate and master's programs at the University of Tennessee.

This pivotal financial support from industry was part of the University of Tennessee's College of Engineering's Bridge to the Future campaign to improve engineering education. Dean of Engineering Bill Snyder and Director of Development Janene Connelly were indispensable to this effort. The authors greatly appreciate their vision and extraordinary effort in supporting this work.

Individuals from the other companies listed were generous

in supporting case-study investigations by students in the engineering course entitled "The Development of Superior Products and Processes." Senior engineers and managers, too numerous to mention here, came to the campus to present their case studies of superior results. Others invited the students to have free access to their engineering and manufacturing people and facilities while giving much more support for the student case studies than was requested. Special thanks go to Phil Faraci and other engineers of Hewlett Packard, San Diego Division, who enabled us to get a view of the HP process of development and manufacturing which are responsible for the vaunted robustness of HP products. Special thanks also go to Jim Mason of Xerox, Tom Abbott of Storage Technology, Greg Survant of Lexmark and my many friends at IBM, Boulder, Lexington and Austin who so generously shared their experiences and wisdom. This encouragement from industry professionals and managers was particularly sustaining to the authors during the early part of the research effort when the academic community did not realize the significance of the program.

We are indebted to the reviewers of this book. Barry Bebb helped us immensely with his superb review of the potential applications for this book, part of which became the foreword to this book. His constructive criticism and thoughtful comments about the product development model were greatly appreciated. Professor Patrick H. Hamilton of the University of Hertfordshire contributed substantially from his point of view as the chairman of the Shared Experience in Engineering Design (SEED) program in England. As a person who has had both substantial industrial and academic experience with engineering design, his detailed comments for each chapter were most useful. Professor Robert Todd of the Manufacturing Engineering Department at Brigham Young University brought his experiences from the engineering practice of product development, manufacturing process development, and his "Integrated Product and Process Design" course to evaluate the text. His comments and suggestions were very helpful.

PREFACE

This book is a summary of what I have learned about product development after a 25-year career in product development and an eight-year research effort. These experiences spanned work on products such as IBM Selectric typewriter products, copiers, and laser printers. Technically, they spanned new technology development to product engineering, manufacturing, and field service assignments. Organizationally, it included working for the smallest division in IBM (the Electric Typewriter Division) as it grew to the largest (the Office Products Division). The organizational structure of this division spanned a totally integrated engineering, manufacturing, sales, and service organization with local management and leadership to the IBM "Big Blue" corporate direction, with its strongly defined functional organizations encouraged to confront each other. For 20 years I held first-, second-, and third-level engineering management positions. I spent two years searching for new ways to improve the quality of products and speed new development after the need to reduce overhead was made abundantly clear by direct competition from the Japanese camera manufacturers who had moved into the copier and laser printer businesses.

The product development research work that is the basis for this book revealed that the problems experienced by IBM were pervasive throughout many US industries. The research was focused to illuminate the successes in the 1980s and 1990s and incorporate them into a set of *essential elements of superior product development* that could be of benefit to industry professionals as well as engineering and business students preparing to move into the field of new product development. The research lessons came from practicing engineers and managers in industry who shared their experiences (both good and bad) while competing for world markets.

Since no one product experience incorporates all of these essential elements and always results in unique "lessons learned," a composite of the favorable experiences has been created in the form of a Product Development Process Model with nine phases defined. We found that successful product development occurs through the integration of contributions of many people from many functional areas and diverse backgrounds. A major task of this integration is for these people to function with mutual respect as an effective team. For this teamwork to happen, there must be understanding of, and respect for, what the other functions have to do. Therefore, a major purpose of the Product Development Process Model is to present a comprehensive overview of the entire process by identifying the *milestone goals* that must be accomplished in each of the phases. We have found this model to be effective in facilitating communication among participants from diverse areas who can quickly identify their own activities while learning about the others.

It is hoped that this model will serve both industry and university environments to facilitate transfer of the essential elements of successful innovative product development. It is the authors' sincere belief that the economic future of our country and our collective standard of living depend upon successful superior product development.

C.C.W.

CHAPTER 1

INTRODUCTION

After trailing in the global marketplace throughout the 1980s, US-based firms now lead in most world markets. American firms still lag, however, with respect to the ability to develop, manufacture, and market technologically innovative products. The product development problem and its proposed solutions are presented in this chapter in sections addressing the following topics:

- The US industrial competitiveness challenge;
- The importance of the product development process;
- Lessons from world-class product development efforts;
- What industry must do to improve the product development process;
- What education must do to prepare students for the product development process; and
- The purpose and organization of this book.

The US Industrial Competitiveness Challenge

During the 1980s, the competitiveness gap between US and foreign competition became truly pervasive; it involved not only general household and small consumer goods but also high-technology products such as copiers, computer memory, and automobiles. Although US-based firms have now regained their world market leadership in most industries, our engineering firms continue to lag behind our Japanese and European competitors in the ability to design and manufacture technologically innovative products. As one General Motors manager acknowledges:

> North American industry is ill prepared for the challenge it will continue to face from foreign competition. Our system of product delivery is inherently flawed and incapable. World class product delivery will be the key

enabler in the battle where quality, cost and speed will determine the survivors [Costello, 1992].

It is easy to find examples of uncompetitive US product costs, excessive development times (the time it takes to turn an idea into a product), and inadequate design and manufacturing capabilities. Consider the following:

- The US-made share of global consumer electronics products declined from almost 100 percent to a mere 5 percent over 30 years [Dertouzos et al., 1989, p.217].
- One firm found that its development time to market was actually three months of work plus nine months of waiting for required management approvals [Brazier and Leonard, 1990, p.53].
- Oldsmobile removed its traditional rocket logo from the new Aurora luxury car after tests showed that customers liked the car much less once they recognized that the vehicle was made by Oldsmobile [Kerwin, 1994].

Comprehensive studies by the MIT Commission on Industrial Productivity and the National Research Council have concluded that many US product development efforts are too slow, too expensive, and too often fail to create products with the features, performance, and quality that customers want.

The Japanese Challenge

The Japanese have issued the loudest wake-up call to US firms. Over the last 20 years, leading Japanese firms have repeatedly demonstrated the ability to develop and manufacture innovative and complex products that combine the best performance, the lowest cost, and the highest quality in the world.

One example of Japanese excellence in product development has been in the automobile industry. Provided with opportunities in the 1970s and 1980s by complacent US automobile makers, Japanese-owned facilities now account for about one-quarter of the automobiles produced in North America. Leadership in this industry is no trivial matter, since motor vehicles account for almost 9 percent of *total* US consumer spending. About 15 percent of the $132.6-*billion* US trade deficit (as of 1993) can be accounted for simply from US net imports of Japanese cars.

Japanese automobile firms have demonstrated that their successes stem from their industrial processes and *not* from their "Japanese culture," as many of those firms now design and manufacture competitive new products entirely within the United States. The fact that these Japanese firms have succeeded after using American workers and after being subject to US domestic constraints demonstrates that the difference is in *how* the firms operate, not *where* they operate.

While American automobile makers focused on high volume and fixed automation, Japanese firms focused on achieving high quality, on meeting the needs of smaller and diverse customer markets, and on developing flexible machines that permitted quick model changeovers. While US firms used a narrowly skilled work force, the Japanese invested in increased capability through company-provided training. While American automobiles were created in sequential fashion by functional experts, Japanese firms deployed teams that guided the new vehicle through the entire product development process. A 1991 study of the worldwide automobile industry concluded that the average US automaker needed 80 percent more engineering hours and 33 percent more development time to create an equivalent vehicle than did the average Japanese firm [Clark and Fujimoto, 1991, pp. 75, 80].

In summary, world-class Japanese firms have not beaten US firms with high technology but rather with basic design and engineering processes and practices. It is the *product development process* that is the key to a resurgence in the ability of American companies to develop technologically innovative products.

The Importance of the Product Development Process

Products and services are the *sine qua non* of a firm; without products and services to offer, a company has no reason to exist. Customers purchase a firm's products only when they find those products to be the most effective in meeting their needs. If a company is to be successful (or even stay in business), its products must be more valuable to their customers than other alternatives – they must be more convenient, more productive, easier to use, and/or less costly. The cover story of the August 1993 issue of *Business Week*, entitled "Flops: Too Many Products Fail . . . ," attests to the general problem of US product development capability.

New products are truly the lifeblood of a company's long-term economic existence. Executives in one survey said that over one-half of their revenues came from sales of products that were not in production ten years ago. The 3M Corporation has a goal to earn at least 40 percent of its annual revenue from products that have been on the market for less than four years.

To be competitive in the future, US product development, manufacturing, and business systems must be substantially improved. Many good design and manufacturing methodologies have been advanced in recent years to improve product quality. Design for assembly (DFA), design for manufacturing (DFM), early manufacturing involvement (EMI), total quality control (TQC), quality circles (QC), quality function deployment (QFD), Taguchi/experimental design methods, computer-aided design (CAD), computer-aided engineering (CAE), computer-aided manufacturing (CAM), and just-in-time manufacturing (JIT) are all worthy methods in an ever-growing list of purported solutions to US product development problems. *Even if these individual methodologies are executed perfectly, however, the resulting products can still fail to win customers.*

This is because the ability of these individual methodologies to improve US product development is limited unless they are used within a coherent *product development process*. The goal cannot be merely to execute the best computer-aided design, the fastest assembly, or the best advertising campaign, but instead must be to create a product that provides the maximum value, robustness, and quality to customers in the shortest possible time. The definition, design, testing, manufacturing, and other activities involved in creating the product must be conducted within the context of an integrated product development process that

4

ensures the control of critical product variables throughout the entire development and manufacturing process.

The difficulties facing US industry are not random events but rather symptoms of systemic problems. Many firms lack a formal process for identifying and controlling key product and process parameters throughout the entire product development process. Some approaches control critical factors through a portion of the product development process, but the effectiveness of these methods is limited. Such approaches are typically not used throughout the entire organization, since they are not an established part of the company's normal operating practice.

Product development is a very complex process that involves the interaction of many activities and personnel. There are large variations in the effectiveness of product development activities among firms, within firms, and even within specific groups within the same firm. These variations in product development process effectiveness can create fatal flaws in the design and/or manufacture of new products.

Lessons from World-Class Product Development Efforts

There are significant differences between successful and mediocre firms. A 1991 McKinsey study indicates that better firms create two and a half times more new products on average than lagging companies. Motorola has found that "best-in-class" firms have error rates 500 to 1,000 times lower than those of average companies.

US Responses to the Competitiveness Challenge

Fortunately, some US firms have responded successfully to the product development challenge presented by world-class competitors, particularly those from Japan. Case studies of innovative product development efforts show that these firms have worked hard to improve their ability to create, design, and manufacture innovative products so that they may survive in an intensely competitive world economy. Operations in these firms are not "business as usual"; in some cases, radical changes to the corporate organization have been required. In all cases, responding firms have made conscious, focused efforts to improve their product development and manufacturing capabilities.

Throughout the last eight years, the authors have studied actual case histories involving the successful development of complex and innovative products. Many of these case histories came from the information products (e.g., copiers, laser printers, transaction recorders, and personal computers) industries, which were among the first during the early 1980s to find that they were no longer competitive with their Japanese counterparts. In response, these firms have changed their product development organizations and processes. Their engineering, manufacturing, and parts purchasing functions have been combined into single teams that value the successful production of a high-quality product over all other functional objectives. The teams operate as small, vertically integrated organizations that include all necessary engineering, manufacturing, and other functions.

Hewlett-Packard was lauded in a September 1994 article in the *Wall Street Journal*. "How H-P Used Tactics of the Japanese to Beat Them at their Own Game" discussed how Hewlett-Packard "grabbed the inkjet-printer market from Japan." The common themes – that is, the elements that contributed most to each product's success – arising from superior product development projects like Hewlett-Packard's series of inkjet printers form the basis for the Product Development Process Model that is presented throughout this book.

The Xerox Example

The Xerox Corporation is frequently held up as an example of a US firm that invented an industry only to lose its dominance after being challenged by a tremendous competitive attack. But in contrast to many American firms that suffered a similar fate, Xerox eventually responded to the challenge and has since regained a significant portion of what it lost. The Xerox case is instructive because it provides key insights into critical challenges that many companies are just now having to face.

As the original inventor of electrophotographic technology, Xerox once enjoyed a near monopoly in the copier market. Because an electrophotographic copier deteriorates as toner (the very fine thermoplastic powder used to create the printed image) contaminates the machine, Xerox products required intensive, expensive service to keep them capable of making clean copies reliably. Some within Xerox refused to see this as a serious problem; in fact, many actually saw the resulting service business (created as the copiers failed from contamination) to be a source of *extra profits!*

Japanese firms targeted the copier market and continuously improved their copiers so that they were more reliable, made superior copies, and required less costly service than did Xerox offerings. With its near monopoly, Xerox had difficulty recognizing that its competitors were now producing superior products. But customers did, and the resulting loss of significant market share came as a shock to the company that "invented the copier business."

Xerox initiated its response to the Japanese challenge in 1980 by comparing (or "benchmarking") itself against its Japanese affiliate, Fuji Xerox. When compared to their Fuji subsidiary, Xerox (1) took twice as long to develop new products; (2) used twice as many people on their development projects; (3) produced comparable products at twice the cost, which meant that Xerox's *production* costs were about as much as Fuji's *selling* costs; and (4) built products with at least twice as many defects. Not only was Xerox (US) seriously behind, but it was losing ground each year: its 8-percent annual productivity improvement rate paled next to Fuji's 14-percent rate of improvement. Not surprisingly, Xerox found itself to be grossly uncompetitive and concluded that it needed to radically improve the way it developed new products.

Xerox's resurgence was a direct result of what it learned from evaluating its product development process against that of its competition. H. Barry Bebb, former Xerox vice president, explains that Xerox reinvented itself by implementing three key decisions:

1. Establishing a clear vision and targets based on competitive benchmarking, with the vision being "to be the first American manufacturing corporation targeted by 'Japan Inc.' to take them on and win," and with targets set to address the discovered shortcomings;

2. Implementing TQM as a core business process; and
3. Implementing concurrent engineering (i.e., establishing integrated product delivery teams organized into business units).

These three key decisions formed the basis for many other initiatives, including establishing competitive benchmarking, involving suppliers early in design, dramatically reducing the number of suppliers (from 5,000 to 500), focusing on customer needs and satisfaction, and replacing inspections in manufacturing processes with statistical process control and quality training for most employees.

What Industry Must Do to Improve the Product Development Process

US industry does not suffer from a dearth of basic science, research results, or prototype development. What it does suffer from is an inability to convert technological discoveries into competitive products – that is, a failure to produce state-of-the-art processes for designing, manufacturing, marketing, and distributing products.

This lack of emphasis on the product development process results in what some call "organizational amnesia," whereby the firm's expertise is dependent solely on individuals (who may go on to other roles or leave the organization altogether) instead of on a systematic, companywide process. Many US firms have declared that shortening the development cycle is critical for future success, but few have defined an *integrated, functionally balanced* product development process to achieve the desired results. Typical ineffective approaches to product development include:

- An overly rigid process characterized by complex, inflexible procedures and costly, time-consuming enforcement mechanisms;
- A group-dominated process where a single group (e.g., marketing, R&D, or manufacturing) is stronger than other functions and dominates decision making; or

- No process at all, which often results in product lacking key customer benefits, erratic organizational performance, and poor product performance.

Improving the product development processes used by American firms is a national imperative for restoring US industrial competitiveness.

The Essential Elements for Superior Product Development

The Product Development Process Model presented in chapter 2 sets out the flow of activities that are needed for achieving superior product development. While the configuration (i.e., the specific form) of the process may differ across organizations, the case studies analyzed by the authors show that four essential elements are needed. They are:

- Control by a single team;
- A vision of the future product;
- A convergence of information from marketing, engineering, and manufacturing; and
- A continuity in the information collected about critical product characteristics.

Sustained market competitiveness requires that a firm create and maintain a superior product development process that includes the essential elements for success. This book provides one such model.

What Education Must Do to Prepare Students for the Product Development Process

The increasing competitiveness of the global marketplace has also led to a reassessment of the educational system that prepares people for work in industry. Many have concluded that changes are needed in how scientists, engineers, managers, and others are educated.

Engineering colleges generally fail to teach the product development process in either the undergraduate or the graduate curriculum. Business schools, too, often do not address the technology and manufacturing challenges related to the development of sophisticated, high-value products. But, as Harvard Business School professor Kim Clark has pointed out, even when these issues are considered, the R&D management principles that are taught arise from "scholars and managers who studied basic laboratories conducting basic research rather than carrying out development projects aimed at immediate commercialization of a product."

Eric Walker, president emeritus and former dean of engineering at Penn State, has described engineering as "a continuing process which begins at the 'bright idea' and invention stage and which continues through development, design, testing, possibly redesign for manufacturing, marketing, selling, and, in many cases, maintenance of the device during its life." A complete engineering education must prepare a student for the total product development process. To accomplish this complete education for both engineering and business students, Dr. John Prados, the 1991 – 92 president of the Accreditation Board for Engineering and Technology, the organization that accredits US university engineering programs, has said that universities need "a much stronger project and case-study orientation, with interdisciplinary teams of engineering and business students working on projects that integrate design, development, manufacturing, and marketing of quality processes and products."

The University of Tennessee's Superior Engineering Design Program

A prototype of the comprehensive experience needed in engineering education has been established in the University of Tennessee's Superior Engineering Design Program (SEDP). Initiated in 1987, the program's mission is to improve the product development teaching and practice so that its graduates can help US industry build world-class products.

In the SEDP, engineering design is taught as a guided, problem-based learning experience. Students, working in teams, develop a product intended for commercial sale or other industrial use. They are directly involved in designing, evaluating, and manufacturing products for the competitive market. Students experience the realistic constraints of schedule, cost, manufacturing, and product performance under the umbrella of the overall product development process presented in this book.

Undergraduate senior design students develop conceptual designs that are built as prototype configurations; production-level designs are implemented and evaluated in the master's program. Related topics and courses cover the Product Development Process Model, which is used to guide students through the development process.

The Purpose, Scope, and Organization of this Book

The *purpose* of this text is to create a comprehensive picture of the total product development process – one that can be used by professionals and students to understand the many different contributions that must be integrated to create a successful new product. By providing a "big picture" of the product development process, the book offers professional specialists and managers, as well as university faculty and students, a broad context for understanding how their expertise contributes to the development of superior products in a competitive environment. In other books that have attempted to address product development, this perspective is often lacking or at best has been limited.

The broader viewpoint provided in this text is increasingly needed to manage the interdisciplinary relationships in a product development effort. For example, the design engineer must understand the needs of the customer so that the product design is optimized from the customer's perspective rather than by arbitrary engineering criteria. Procurement staff need to realize how their practices affect whether the manufacturing facility functions as expected and how quickly it can be completed. Process developers need to know what design characteristics are the most critical for achieving desired product performance. Suppliers, marketing and sales staff, safety experts, lawyers, distributors, and many other employees also contribute their expertise. The book can be used to bridge the language gap that often exists between functions by helping all to understand their relative roles, capabilities, and information needs.

This book can be used by both engineering and business faculty to incorporate new product development into existing courses or to form the basis for a new course. Engineering faculty for upper-division undergraduate and graduate courses can use the text as a foundation for adding real product development experience to the design curriculum.

The *scope* of this text directly encompasses the several classes of electronic, mechanical, and software products upon which the book is based. These desktop electronic products (e.g., computers, laser printers, and typewriters), vehicles, appliances, and associated products of discrete manufacture have created the foundation from which the concepts presented in the book have been developed.

Of course, no product development model can be made to fit every product development effort in every industry. The essential elements of the model, however, can serve as a foundation for establishing or improving the product development process of small, medium, or large firms and for training students in the fundamentals of sound product development practice.

The book's *organization* provides a progression through the development process. Chapter 1 explains why the product development process is so important to US industrial competitiveness. Chapter 2 provides an overview of the Product Development Process Model, a synthesis of the essential elements of superior practice as identified from the authors' research on successful product development case studies.

Chapters 3 through 10 present the phases of the Product Development Process Model. Each phase is presented in the following format.

- The *Milestone Goals* section describes the goals for the phase.
- The *Process Description* section defines what occurs during the phase.
- The *Essential Elements* section defines the invariant characteristics of the phase – that is, the things that must

happen regardless of an organization's particular implementation of the activities in the phase.
- The *Summary* defines the work products and results that are produced during the phase.

For instructors and students, discussion questions for chapters 3 through 10 are provided in an appendix.

Summary

The US product development competitiveness problem is multifaceted. Its aspects cover the entire scope of product development – from finding and selecting the product idea to sustained manufacturing. As once-dominant American firms find their new product development capabilities to be inadequate, many will attempt to solve their problems through massive organizational restructuring. Experience has shown, however, that firms that focus on *improving their product development processes* are more likely to be successful in creating high-value, robust, timely products that are successful from both a technical and a marketing standpoint.

References

Brazier, David, and Mike Leonard, "Concurrent Engineering: Participating in Better Designs," *Mechanical Engineering*, January 1990, pp. 52-53.

Clark, Kim B., and Takahiro Fujimoto (1991), *Product Development Performance: Strategy, Organization, and Management in the World Auto Industry*, Harvard Business School Press, Boston.

Costello, Tim (1992), "Benchmarking the World's 'Product Delivery Systems'," Presentation to the How To Implement Concurrent Engineering Conference, Society of Manufacturing Engineers, Detroit, MI, May 5-6, 1992.

Dertouzos, Michael L., et al. and the MIT Commission on Industrial Productivity (1989), *Made in America – Regaining the Productive Edge*, The MIT Press, Cambridge, MA.

Kerwin, Kathleen (1994), "GM's Aurora," *Business Week*, March 21, 1994, pp. 88-95.

Selected Bibliography

Hadden, L. L. (1986), "Product Development at Xerox: Meeting the Competitive Challenge," notes from presentation to Copying and Duplicating Industry Conference, February 10 – 12, 1986.

National Research Council (1991), *Improving Engineering Design: Designing for Competitive Advantage*, Washington, DC.

Power, Christopher, et al. (1993), "Flops: Too Many New Products Fail. Here's Why – and How To Do Better," *Business Week*, August 16, 1993, pp. 76 – 82.

Prados, John (1992), "Engineering Design: The *Sine Qua Non* of Engineering Education," ABET President 1991 – 92, Chemical Engineering Department, The University of Tennessee, Knoxville.

Speckhart, Frank H., and Clement C. Wilson (1991), "Product Development in the University Environment," *Proceedings of International Design Productivity Conference (Vol. 1)*, Honolulu, HI, February 1991.

Speckhart, Frank H., and Clement C. Wilson (1993), "Beyond the ABET Requirements: A Progress Report on a Five-Year Effort to Improve Engineering Design," *Innovations in Engineering Design Education Resource Guide*, compendium to the 1993 ASME Design Education Conference, Orlando, FL: March 1993, pp. 121 – 24.

Walker, Eric (1989), "Engineering Schools Share the Blame for Declining Productivity," *The Bent of Tau Beta Pi*, Spring 1989, pp. 12 – 14.

Xerox Corporation (1990), *The Xerox Quest for Quality and the National Quality Award*, Xerox Corporation, Rochester, NY.

Yoder, Stephen Kreider (1994), "How H-P Used Tactics of the Japanese to Beat Them at Their Own Game," *The Wall Street Journal*, September 8, 1994, pp. A1, A9.

CHAPTER 2

THE PRODUCT DEVELOPMENT PROCESS

This chapter gives the reader a foundation for understanding the product development process. It presents an overview of the Product Development Process Model, outlines the essential elements of successful implementation, and discusses how product development techniques can be put in practice.

The Product Development Process Model is made up of nine distinct phases that deal with:

- Product ideas;
- Customer future needs projection;
- Product technology selection and development;
- Process technology selection and development;
- Final product definition and project targets;
- Product marketing and distribution preparation;
- Product design and evaluation;
- Manufacturing system design; and
- Product manufacture, delivery, and use.

The discussion of the essential elements of successful implementation will include the following topics:

- Control by a single team;
- A vision of the future product;
- The convergence of information from marketing, engineering, and manufacturing; and
- A continuity of information about critical product characteristics.

An Overview of the Product Development Process Model

The Product Development Process Model for innovative products portrayed in figure 2.1 is based on lessons learned from case studies of leading US firms that are competing successfully against world-class competitors, particularly those from Japan.

The process occurs in nine major phases, originating with the Product Ideas phase and concluding with the Product Manufacture, Delivery, and Use phase. Work on the marketing, engineering, and manufacturing aspects of the process takes place concurrently during product planning and converges in the Final Product Definition and Project Targets phase. Similarly, marketing, engineering, and manufacturing activities are concurrent during product execution and are reintegrated in the Product Manufacturing, Delivery, and Use phase.

Each development phase has a "milestone goal" that defines the completion of that phase, as indicated by the numbered flags in figure 2.1. Major management phase reviews occur in conjunction with the completion of the milestone goals. These phase reviews are comprehensive and include all engineering, financial, manufacturing, marketing, and distribution considerations. (The term "phase review" is used in this book to describe major management reviews.)

The introduction to the Product Development Process Model in this chapter provides an overview of each phase. More detailed descriptions of the phases of the process are given in chapters 3 through 10.

Product Ideas

The milestone goal for the Product Ideas phase of product development is the creation of "high-value" product concepts that are consistent with the firm's strategic goals. High-value ideas are those that provide distinctive customer benefits relative to the competition. A successful product will have some features that can immediately be identified as the characteristics that makes the product superior to existing products.

Product ideas are generated from external sources (e.g.,

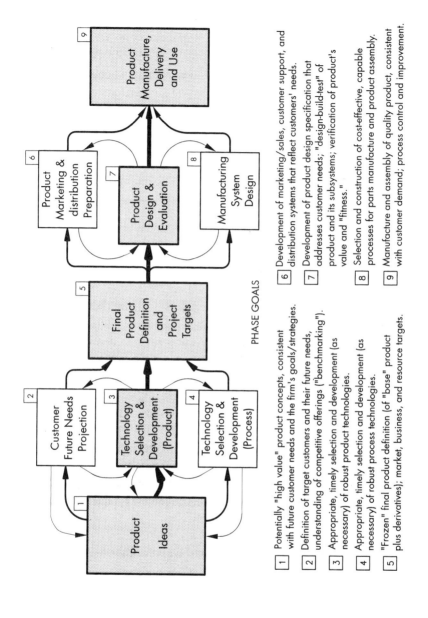

Figure 2.1. A Superior Product Development Process for an innovative product, with milestone goals for each phase.

PHASE GOALS

1. Potentially "high value" product concepts, consistent with future customer needs and the firm's goals/strategies.
2. Definition of target customers and their future needs, understanding of competitive offerings ("benchmarking").
3. Appropriate, timely selection and development (as necessary) of robust product technologies.
4. Appropriate, timely selection and development (as necessary) of robust process technologies.
5. "Frozen" final product definition (of "base" product plus derivatives); market, business, and resource targets.
6. Development of marketing/sales, customer support, and distribution systems that reflect customers' needs.
7. Development of product design specification that addresses customer needs; "design-build-test" of product and its subsystems; verification of product's value and "fitness."
8. Selection and construction of cost-effective, capable processes for parts manufacture and product assembly.
9. Manufacture and assembly of quality product, consistent with customer demand; process control and improvement.

customers, advertising agencies, suppliers, and inventors) or internal sources (e.g., the marketing staff, the R&D staff, the sales force, corporate planning groups, or newly acquired businesses). Ideas may arise as unsolicited suggestions or through planned idea-generation activities. Planned idea generation occurs through the systematic consideration of possibilities such as addressing customer wishes or complaints, customizing an existing product, and using manufacturing by-products. Product ideas are screened against factors such as internal capabilities, technical feasibility, and financial risk.

Customer Future Needs Projection

The milestone goal for the Customer Future Needs Projection phase *is the projection of high-value product ideas over a future time period.* New products must be defined in terms of the customers' future requirements as well as their current needs.

The projection of high-value ideas means identifying the window of future market opportunity, from product introduction through the end of production. Key activities required to make such a projection are quantifying the customer's definition of product quality, assessing the characteristics of the market, and analyzing the ability of the competition.

A product of high value relative to future customer needs, developed within a defined window of market opportunity, must ultimately be characterized in terms of the optimal combination of the highest product performance, the lowest product cost, and the fastest possible development time.

Product Technology Selection and Development

The milestone goal for the Product Technology Selection and Development phase is the selection of appropriate, robust product technologies. Such technologies will meet customers' expectations, work properly in a product environment, and be manufacturable with high yields. The technologies selected may or may not be the latest, but they will be the most appropriate ones for the product.

Technologies must be selected that will meet the customer's expectation for product performance. Quality measures must be defined for assessing and comparing the technologies, and just enough information must be generated to be able to make good decisions. Both current and new technologies are candidates for consideration, and comparative tests, experiments, and simulations must be performed to evaluate the candidate technologies. In particular, the controlling variables must be identified and tested over a range of conditions that is adequate to confirm function in the required "operating space" (the intersection of performance requirements).

Technologies are assessed relative to performance on customer requirements, technical barriers, cost, and relation to the firm's competence. The specific final result of the phase is a Technology Feasibility Statement, which sets forth:

- Critical performance parameters and a description of the required operating space;
- Any major limitations to design, use, and manufacture;
- Special materials or manufacturing processes required; and
- Explicit confirmation that a working configuration with needed instrumentation and controls has been successfully tested.

The first major management phase review, which occurs at the end of this process, is called the Technical Feasibility Phase Review. This review includes the results of the Process Technology Selection and Development phase.

Process Technology Selection and Development

The milestone goal for the Process Technology Selection and Development phase is the selection of appropriate, robust process technologies. New process technologies should be developed simultaneously and in conjunction with new product technologies. The requirements and limitations of each affect the design considerations of the other.

Design and manufacturing engineers should be physically located at the same site to facilitate the teamwork that is critical to concurrent engineering. The product design must reflect manufacturing, automation, and assembly considerations from the very beginning. Early involvement of vendors can also enable adjustments to be made on a short cycle and thus ensure ultimate manufacturability.

The Process Technology Selection and Development activities parallel the Product Technology Selection and Development activities just described and result in a Technology Feasibility Statement for manufacturing process technology.

Final Product Definition and Project Targets

The milestone goal for the Final Product Definition and Project Targets phase is the establishment of a set of strategic product and project targets. These targets result from the convergence of marketing, engineering, and manufacturing information and include (1) specifications for the product "family" (i.e., the base product and anticipated derivative products), and (2) the market, budget, schedule, and staffing targets for the project.

The Product Concept Phase Review ensures that the targets proposed that define the product and project plans are supported appropriately by management.

Product Marketing and Distribution Preparation

The milestone goal for the Product Marketing and Distribution Preparation phase is a product introduction plan. This includes a marketing plan that identifies sales channels, promotional methods, and pricing structure and a distribution plan that spells out the logistics of ordering, shipping, and billing.

Product Design and Evaluation

The milestone goals for the Product Design and Evaluation phase are the definition of the product architecture; the design, construction, and testing of subassemblies; and testing of the integrated system.

A formal Product Design Specification (PDS) is completed before design begins. The PDS is a comprehensive report on the major features, uses, and expected usage conditions for the product. The PDS includes descriptions of:

- The product's characteristics (e.g., its features, performance, size, and weight);
- The life of the product (e.g., its competitive life span or shelf life);
- Customer use (e.g., installation, maintenance, disposal, and documentation);
- Product development considerations (e.g., time, environment, materials, and safety);
- Manufacturing factors (e.g., facilities, processes, quantity, and packaging); and
- A definition of the market and a marketing plan (e.g., customer identification, competitive assessment, and market window).

A design readiness review is held after the PDS has been prepared. When the team is satisfied that the PDS is complete, design begins.

The product design should be robust; it should accommodate a worst-case scenario for parts and environment. The critical functional and manufacturing parameters should be described in formal product documentation and should be well understood by all team members.

The performance of the product should be certified in a comprehensive test program. The product should be tested under both routine and nonroutine operating conditions. Deliberate failure evaluation (stress testing) should be performed to ensure that the product will operate under worst-case customer usage conditions.

The product design and evaluation phase is concluded with the Product Release Review, which verifies that the new product has indeed been engineered and tested properly and will meet the requirements of the Product Design Specification, the business plan targets, and – of course – the customer.

Manufacturing System Design

The milestone goal for the Manufacturing System Design phase is the selection and implementation of cost-effective, capable manufacturing and assembly processes. Critical process technologies should be controlled internally by the company or controlled *very* closely with preferred suppliers.

Standard, well-understood processes should be selected for the manufacturing system. Process feasibility should be demonstrated using a manual procedure, with automation introduced only after processes are stable.

Criteria for the movement of the product into the manufacturing process are established during the Manufacturing System Design phase. A Manufacturing Readiness Review is held as the final step in the phase to confirm that the criteria have been met.

Product Manufacture, Delivery, and Use

The milestone goal for the final phase, Product Manufacture, Delivery, and Use, is the ongoing manufacture and delivery of quality products. Processes are controlled through statistical process control and are continuously improved by the manufacturing team.

The final management review prior to launching the product is the Product Launch Readiness Review. The final review of product performance to ensure customer delight is the Product Infant Mortality Tracking Program Review.

The Essential Elements of Successful Implementation

The Product Development Process Model is a general characterization of the flow of work in new product development. Organizations may use a variety of management and technical methods in the process with success, as long as the *essential* elements for success are present. The essential elements for the successful implementation of each phase of the product development process will be presented in subsequent chapters, but four of these elements are so fundamental that they must be emphasized at the outset. The remainder of this chapter summarizes and discusses these four elements, which are:

- Control by a single team;
  - Team integrates broad skills needed to develop product; and
  - Team controls all aspects, from technology selection to manufacturing.
- Creation of a vision for the future product;
  - Projection of customers' future needs;
  - Team participates directly in future needs projection; and
  - Customers provide direct input to team members.
- Information convergence at the Product Definition phase; and
  - Team considers all critical issues early and simultaneously; and
  - Team establishes common goals and plans via consensus.
- Information continuity for critical product characteristics.

Control by a Single Team

First among the four essential elements for successful product development is the selection of a single marketing/engineering/manufacturing team to control the project from technology selection through the first six months of manufacturing.

The Xerox Corporation uses a "product delivery team" that reports to a chief engineer. When IBM could not produce a personal computer using its formal product development system, it commissioned an "independent business unit" – a small team with complete autonomy to develop the machine. Hewlett-Packard used the team approach to develop its color Paintjet printer. These major companies, who are competing directly against the Japanese, have found that matrix organizations, with their built-in turf battles and lack of responsibility for the product, are not competitive against Japanese cooperative systems. Figure 2.2 illustrates how the parochial interests of the traditional matrix organization cause the

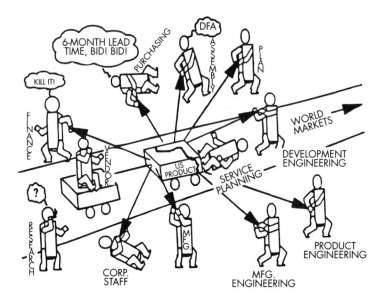

Figure 2.2. The "traditional" US product development system fosters "inaction."

product to be sabotaged by the very people who are supposed to be ensuring its success. Xerox's Lyndon Hadden has stated that the previous product delivery system was a "system created to prevent errors . . . but [it] almost prevented product delivery." The single, functionally integrated product development team (illustrated in figure 2.3) is the most essential element for superior product development.

If a single team is to be responsible for the product throughout the development process, its members must posess the proper mix of skills and experience to do the job. Various team members need to have the design, manufacturing, marketing, testing, and other skills necessary to develop the product successfully. The most effective teams have a single leader with the authority to control *all* aspects of the project, from the technology selection phase through the first six months of product manufacture.

The Honda Accord is a good example of a highly successful

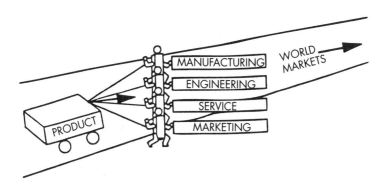

Figure 2.3. The "new" US product development system "in action."

product controlled by a single team. When the team was first assembled in 1986, a "large project leader" was assigned who borrowed personnel from various departments and transferred them to the Accord team for the life of the project. A "basic car" team was assigned to develop the base vehicle, and two subteams were named to customize the base vehicle body for international market segments. The functional specialists on the team worked with their functional departments but reported to the large project leader. The Accord was launched in late 1989, roughly three years after the start of the project.

Studies summarizing the characteristics of effective project teams cite the following important factors:

- Co-location of team members;
- Mechanisms for informal communication;
- Training for team building;
- Leadership based on team facilitation;
- Delegation of decision authority to the lowest possible level; and
- Performance measurement based on team measures.

25

Vision of the Future Product

The second essential element affecting the entire development process is the existence of a product "vision" that sustains the team's momentum throughout the life of the project. A guiding vision of the ability of the product to meet customers' future needs can create an enthusiasm and dedication that contribute immeasurably to the achievement of the project's goals.

The product vision is created during the Customer Future Needs Projection phase of the product development process. It is the team's window to the future throughout the project. The team should participate directly in the determination of customer needs. Team participation can enhance team members' creative contributions by enabling them to "see" opportunities that they might overlook if they merely read a report from a distant market analysis group.

Team interaction with customers should continue throughout the development process. One data storage firm established a customer advisory board to provide direct customer involvement during the design process. The board is composed of technically astute customers, such as data center directors and systems engineers. New product designs are discussed with board members to provide them with advance notice of new products and to solicit suggestions for product improvements. Design engineers attend these meetings to answer questions and receive direct feedback from customers.

Direct and ongoing interaction between team members and customers is an essential element in successful development of innovative products. The initial product vision arises from understanding customers' future needs, and the team's momentum is sustained through reinforcement of the product vision in continuing customer contact.

The Convergence of Information from Marketing, Engineering, and Manufacturing

The minimum possible product development time is enabled by a process consisting of the maximum possible concurrent activity. Carefully planned convergence of marketing, engineering,

and manufacturing information is absolutely essential to effective concurrency in the development process.

While ongoing consultation and feedback occur between functional activities throughout product development, the explicit convergence of marketing, engineering, and manufacturing information occurs twice in the Product Development Process Model portrayed in figure 2.1. The convergence of planning information occurs at the Final Product Definition and Project Targets phase, and the convergence of development information takes place during the Product Manufacturing, Delivery, and Use phase.

Early, simultaneous consideration of marketing, engineering, and manufacturing issues must result in the project leaders' agreement on a common set of product targets. The product market opportunity must be reflected in the product design specification, which must in turn be supported by appropriate manufacturing process technologies. Agreement among the project leaders enables parallel product and process development to occur with minimum conflict. If common targets are not developed at the outset, the concurrent engineering of product and process is likely to result in major product and process rework late in the development process, lengthy project delays, and even project failure.

The final convergence of marketing, engineering, and manufacturing information must confirm that plans were executed as intended, that projections are still valid, and that all systems are ready for product launch. Specific confirmation is needed that the product as designed meets the criteria for the product as specified, and that the product as manufactured will meet the established targets.

A Continuity of Information about Critical Product Characteristics

Quantitative measures for critical product characteristics must be developed at the start of the product development process and used throughout the process for product quality "scorekeeping." Some of the ways in which these measures can be used in the various development phases are illustrated in figure 2.4.

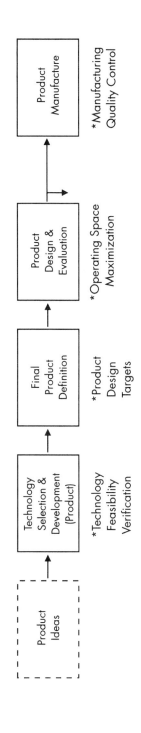

Figure 2.4. Selected phases from figure 2.1, illustrating how measurements of critical product characteristics are used throughout the entire product development process.

(The selected product development phases shown are extracted from figure 2.1.)

The selection and development of suitable measures for critical product characteristics is a difficult task and must be a planned, deliberate activity. Since product characteristics vary widely, measurement criteria and techniques also differ. However, some common elements of superior product characteristic measures clearly distinguish them from other, less effective measures. Superior product measures are:

- Customer oriented;
  - Measures are characteristics that are important to customers; and
  - Quantified limits are derived from customer participation.
- Developed at the start of the process through a planned activity;
- Simple and easy to use; and
- Measures have multiple uses throughout the development process.
  - Measures are used for product quality scorekeeping; and
  - Measures are used to measure and assess the development program.

The best product measures are customer-oriented in at least two ways: the measures quantify characteristics that are important to customers, and acceptable values for these measurements are based on direct customer input. Even subjective characteristics are measured, as necessary, if those items are important to the customer. The most effective measures are simple, effective, and easy to use.

In one major laser printer development project, measures were developed for the important, subjective characteristic called "print quality." Customer surveys were used to establish print quality requirements for the products. The print quality measures were used to verify technology feasibility, to define product design targets and specifications, and to set production quality requirements. The respective development teams used print quality measures to assess how well they were doing throughout the entire product development process.

The structure of many US companies makes it difficult to ensure that important information related to critical product characteristics is transferred to – and understood by – the manufacturing organization. The single, functionally integrated teams in superior projects carry critical product information into the manufacturing phase, since the team is responsible for manufacturing system design and pilot manufacturing.

In one case study involving the development of a typewriter keyboard, the production team defined a formal method for transferring critical product characteristic information to the manufacturing process. This transfer formally connected development to manufacturing and serves as an outstanding example of how product quality can be improved by ensuring the continuity of critical product information throughout the development process. This example is described in the following paragraphs and is illustrated in figure 2.5.

Keyboard "touch" is an important product feature for typewriters and personal computers; it is often the deciding factor in a new product purchase. Therefore, the force-deflection characteristic for the keys, which determines their "touch," is a critical product characteristic for keyboard design.

Steps 1 through 3 of figure 2.5 illustrate how this characteristic is identified, quantified, and designed. The characteristic is then documented in the product engineering specification as a "critical-to-function" (CTF) parameter that must be controlled (step 4). Part dimensions and features that affect the critical-to-function parameter subsequently are identified as CTF dimensions on the engineering drawings. In step 5, some of the CTF dimensions are designated as process control dimensions (PCDs) to be used for manufacturing process control. Statistical process control (SPC) is implemented in manufacturing (step 6) using the PCDs to ensure that the process is stable and capable of making a product that will meet all engineering specification requirements. To ensure manufacturing adherence to engineering specifications, any off-specification permit for a CTF dimen-

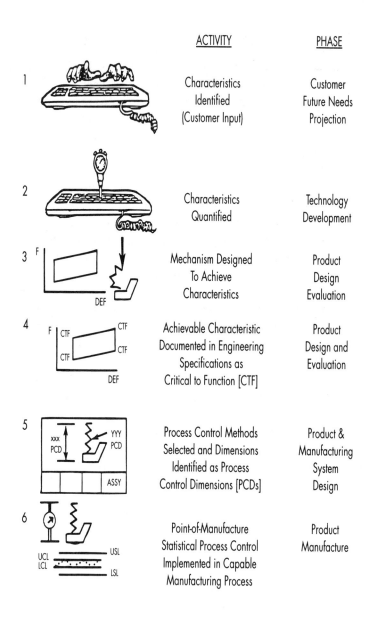

		ACTIVITY	PHASE
1		Characteristics Identified (Customer Input)	Customer Future Needs Projection
2		Characteristics Quantified	Technology Development
3		Mechanism Designed To Achieve Characteristics	Product Design Evaluation
4		Achievable Characteristic Documented in Engineering Specifications as Critical to Function [CTF]	Product Design and Evaluation
5		Process Control Methods Selected and Dimensions Identified as Process Control Dimensions [PCDs]	Product & Manufacturing System Design
6		Point-of-Manufacture Statistical Process Control Implemented in Capable Manufacturing Process	Product Manufacture

Figure 2.5. Illustration of a formal method for transferring critical product characteristic information into the manufacturing

31

sion requires the written, signed approval of the third-level manufacturing manager.

Converting CTF parameters into PCDs for statistical control of the manufacturing process is a powerful technique. It is a documented, formal method for transferring the necessary information so that critical product characteristics can be controlled properly throughout the entire product development process.

Product Development in Practice

Two key challenges pervade the Product Development Process Model: customer orientation and cross-functional integration.

Customer orientation can be maintained through two of the four essential elements described in this chapter: a vision of a product that will meet the customer's future needs and customer-oriented measures of product quality that are tracked throughout product development. Cross-functional integration is possible through the other two essential elements in this chapter: control of the project by a single team and the explicit convergence of marketing, engineering, and manufacturing information in the process model.

This chapter provides the foundation for an understanding of a very complex process. The four essential elements of successful implementation of the Product Development Process Model discussed in this chapter are necessary, but not sufficient in and of themselves, for superior product development. The individual phases of the process and the essential elements of their implementation are put into practice in chapters 3 through 10.

Selected Bibliography

Abbott, Tom (1988), "Improving the Product Development Process," notes from ASME short course, "Case Studies of Engineering and Manufacturing Methods for Superior Results," Atlanta, GA, April 18 – 19, 1988.

Hadden, L. Lyndon (1986), "Product Development at Xerox: Meeting the Competitive Challenge," notes from a presentation to the Copying and Duplicating Industry Conference, February 10 – 12, 1986.

McLeod, G., et al. (1989), Interviews with Hewlett-Packard Plotter Pen and Paintjet teams, San Diego, CA, May 1989.

Pollard, Ed (1989), "IBM Typewriter Keyboard Design," notes from a case study presented at the University of Tennessee, Knoxville, TN, September 26, 1989.

Wilson, Clement C., and Michael E. Kennedy (1989a), "Some Essential Elements For Superior Product Development," ASME Winter Annual Meeting, San Francisco, CA, December 1989.

Wilson, Clement C., and Michael E. Kennedy (1989b), "Quantification of Critical Product Characteristics for Superior Product Development," ASME Winter Annual Meeting, San Francisco, CA, December 1989.

CHAPTER 3

PRODUCT IDEAS

While the need to make products "valuable" may be obvious, defining exactly *what* is valuable in a product certainly is not. Customer needs and value opinions are not static; they change over time, sometimes dramatically. Occasionally a new product makes existing ones much less valuable than before, or even obsolete. Consider how few long-playing records are bought now that customers can purchase CDs instead. In other cases, customers do not even really know what they need; they only realize their need once a solution appears in the form of a new product. How many of the now millions of "post-it note" users could have described this product before it actually existed?

Even if customer needs were always well known and never changed, product development would be challenging enough, for the engineering efforts necessary to turn a concept into a working and reliable product are substantial. (These efforts are defined in subsequent chapters.) But because customer needs do change, a product development process must, at a minimum, *accommodate* these changes. However, a superior development process *predicts* changes in customer needs and takes advantage of them to create products of exceptional value.

Thus, the first steps in the superior product development process are to identify the customers' needs and to develop ideas for products to meet these needs. These activities are performed throughout the Product Ideas and the Customer Future Needs Projection phases.

Milestone Goal

The milestone goal for the Product Ideas phase is *to create and select high-customer-value product concepts*. High-value product concepts provide superior solutions to customer needs throughout the product's entire market life. These concepts also provide value to the company by helping it achieve its strategic goals and objectives.

Process Description

The Product Ideas phase, illustrated in figure 3.1, is the first phase of the product development process for an innovative product. Product concepts emerging from the Product Ideas phase are advanced to the Customer Future Needs Projection and the Technology Selection and Development phases so that customer needs and technology issues can be investigated concurrently. The Product Ideas phase is addressed in this chapter; the Customer Future Needs Projection phase is considered in chapter 4.

Major tasks associated with the Product Ideas phase are shown in figure 3.2. During this phase, ideas from a wide variety of sources are generated or identified and a potential product is defined. This is called an initial Product Concept Description. These product ideas are evaluated, or "screened," against many criteria related to customers and their needs, markets, technology, and the strategic needs of the firm itself. The product ideas that are found to be worthy of development effort are used to create an enhanced Product Concept Description.

Essential Elements

The essential elements for the Product Ideas phase encourage the team to stay focused on the needs of the customer and on using the competitive strengths of the organization. These elements are:

- The product has *significant points of difference* from competition;
- There is a focus on *customer benefits* of the product; and
- The concept is *compatible* with the organization.

"Significant points of difference" refers to the need for any product to have some characteristic, feature, or other distin-

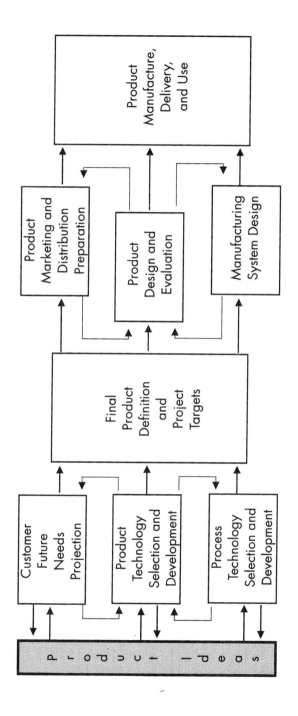

Figure 3.1. The Product Ideas phase within the overall product development process.

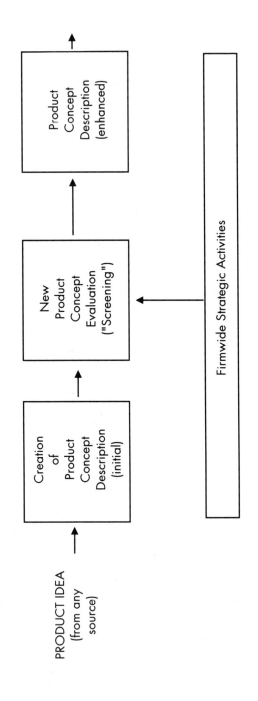

Figure 3.2. The Product Ideas phase.

guishing aspect that can be immediately recognized by customers as making it superior to existing products. These points of difference are the major focus of attention throughout the development process; they are often featured in the marketing campaign.

A team focus on the product's customer benefits is needed to complete the major task of the Product Ideas phase: to determine the specific customer benefits that are to be provided from possessing or using the product. Any focus on specific features or performance is limited to those that are inherently related to such customer benefits.

Better ideas or concepts are usually said to be "compatible" with the organization that is charged to develop them when they are able to make as much use as possible of the firm's competitive advantages. However, there are some dramatic counterexamples in which new products were stymied within large organizations due to their incompatibility with a corporate strategy. In some of those cases, key employees resigned and started competitive businesses, much to the detriment of the original corporation. Perhaps one of the most beneficial things that IBM has done for the US economy was to refuse to develop some of their employees' product ideas. As a result, many successful businesses have been started by ex-IBMers based around such products as Amdahl mainframes, Seagate disk drives, and Storage Technology tape drives.

Creating and Identifying Product Ideas

A group enters the Product Ideas phase with either a product idea or the need to develop one. If the goal is to identify some ideas, the key question is "How can good product ideas be located and identified?" Once an idea is put forth, the major components of this product, in terms of its benefits or value to customers, have to be identified.

Generating Product Ideas

Product ideas may arise from a multitude of sources, but in general they can be categorized as being either "internal" or "external" to the firm. Internal idea sources reside within the firm itself; they include the marketing personnel, R&D engineers, and planning groups. If the company's product line is sold through a sales force that has direct contact with the product's users, such people can be useful sources of information about the customers' needs and their dissatisfaction with current products, if any.

External sources of product ideas include customers, supplier firms, and outside inventors who may approach the firm with ideas for new products. Customer comments and complaints about the firm's products, in particular, can be used as a basis for generating ideas for improving those products. Externally generated product ideas can also be collected from structured customer contacts, such as those made through focus groups.

Ideas can result from formal idea-generation activities, or they may be arrived at spontaneously. "Planned" ideas are generated through a systematic consideration of available information, such as analyzing customer suggestions and complaints, investigating potential uses of manufacturing by-products, or brainstorming potential ways to customize one of the firm's existing products. "Accidental" ideas may arise from such things as unintended laboratory discoveries or a casual customer comment. One of the most beneficial product ideas in the office product industry was initiated when engineer Ron Davidge asked his wife, a secretary, for an idea to improve typewriters. She said: "Make it erase." Although it took another five years to develop the technology of the erasing Selectric typewriter, the idea was initiated by a user of the product who expressed the vision of what was needed. Better firms use both methods; they attempt to generate ideas through planned activities while remaining on constant lookout for any serendipitous opportunities that may appear.

The Initial Product Concept Description

The purpose of the Product Concept Description phase is to state succinctly the basic objectives and intentions of the new product.

Initially, the product description should answer four basic questions pertaining to the product idea:

- What are the product's essential features and functions?
- Who are the product's customers and what are their applications?
- What are the product's essential benefits to the customers?
- When is the product needed?

To answer the first question, the team describes the critical tasks to be performed by the product. These tasks are identified as actions and are described using verbs rather than nouns. They are seen from the customer's perspective. Thus, the team would want to answer "To communicate written business documents from one business location to another" rather than "a facsimile machine." At this point, a sketch of the product – even if it is only a sketch of boxes and telephone lines – can be very helpful in illustrating the concept.

"Whom does the product serve?" defines the product's target customers and users. Key characteristics of these customers are also described. If the persons who purchase the product and the persons who use the product are not the same, then these differences are identified.

"What are the product's essential benefits?" attempts to capture the reasons why customers will need the proposed product. What needs now exist (or will exist) that can be satisfied by the proposed product? What benefits (e.g., cost or time savings) will the customer achieve?

In addition to these basic questions, the team should also answer several "when" questions related to the need for the product, including:

- Does the need for the product exist now, or does the product address a future need?
- When will customers sense a need for the product?
- How long will the identified need continue to exist?

Types of New Products

An important step toward understanding a proposed new product is to know what type of product it is. The product's type will affect not only how much work and time will be needed to complete its development but what its market potential (i.e., its potential sales) might be. As we have also noted, a different set of criteria should usually be used when evaluating different types of products. Major product types based on definitions developed by Steven Wheelright are shown in table 3.1.

Product types that lead to more difficult products and longer development projects appear in the left column while types needing shorter development efforts appear in the right. The reward for pursuing higher risk projects, of course, is that if new markets are created, sales and profits are generally much larger.

As shown in table 3.1, most product types can be categorized under two major headings based on their level of difficulty and market potential: "base" (or "core") products and "derivative" products.

Table 3.1. Major product types.

More Lengthy Projects Core or Base Products	Less Lengthy Projects Derivative Products
Breakthrough	Customized
Platform	Enhanced
	Hybrid
	Cost-reduced

Base Products.   Base products provide customers with entirely new or significantly higher benefits than other alternatives. Base products consist of two primary types: "breakthrough" products and "platform" products.

Breakthrough products are fundamentally different from all other products in some substantial way and generally require the use of new product technologies, concepts, and/or processes to attain their superior capabilities. Examples of breakthrough products would include the first plain-paper copier and the first facsimile machine.

Platform products are the results of fundamental improvements in cost, quality, and general performance over previous generations of similar products. Usually, new platforms meet the needs of general customers, but also are designed so that other somewhat modified products can be created easily from that model. It is the first, standard model to be produced. (The following products are derivatives.)

An example of a platform product is Intel's initial 80486 microprocessor, which is used in many desktop computers. This chip has significantly higher performance versus previous similar products (such as the 80386 chip), and has been used as a "base" (or a "platform") for a number of other, "derivative" products (such as the 486SX, 486-25, 486-33, 486-50, etc.). New platform products include the cab-forward, front-wheel-drive automobiles of the Chrysler Corporation, which have been very well received by the public.

Derivative Products. As suggested above, derivative products are generally versions of a base product that are modified to meet more specific customer needs. These modifications fall into four general categories: customized, enhanced, cost reduced, and hybrid.

A "customized" product is a base product that has been modified specifically for a particular customer, distributor, or retailer. Such modifications can range from the simple addition of a custom logo to more complex changes in features or performance. Adding new, distinctive features or higher performance to a base product creates an enhanced product, for example. These products attract customers who desire, and are willing to pay for, more features or need higher performance than the standard product.

The "cost-reduced" derivative often contains fewer features or lower performance than the base product. These lower-priced versions attract price-sensitive customers who do not require the full performance of the base product. Cost-reduced versions are often created after the base product is introduced by making design or manufacturing improvements that reduce the cost of the base product.

"Hybrid" products combine aspects of two or more base

products, the end result of which is a product that lies in between them.

The "innovative products" that we refer to throughout this book generally refer to product types in the breakthrough and platform products in the base category. Very simple derivative products may not need to proceed through the entire process that we describe in this book.

Evaluating Product Ideas

Once an idea is defined, activities begin to answer the question "Is this an idea that the firm should develop into a new product?" The answer to this question is obtained by evaluating, or screening, the idea against multiple criteria that are expected to affect the potential success of the product.

Objectives

The basic goals of the idea evaluation process are threefold: (1) to have a timely, efficient, and balanced evaluation of proposed new product concepts; (2) to reject poor concepts before spending significant resources in evaluating them or in actually developing the idea; and (3) to avoid rejecting solid concepts that should actually be pursued.

Essentially, screening is used to decide which product ideas merit additional development. Thus, the team wants to investigate the *most significant* issues pertaining to the idea *just enough* to decide whether the idea should proceed to the next product development phases (i.e., the Customer Future Needs Projection and Technology Selection and Development phases) or should not be pursued.

Guidelines for Use

Common sense as well as a formal study [Duerr, 1986, p.4] suggests that the effectiveness of a screening process used to select ideas is not based on the formality of that process. In other words, a complex, written procedure is not necessarily better than a more informal process; in fact, rigid procedures can be less effective by forcing groups to spend more time and resources than necessary. Instead, any screening process that utilizes a clear understanding of the customers' needs and the firm's objectives, capabilities, and limitations can be effective.

Whatever idea evaluation method is used by the team should be defined adequately and agreed to by all important stakeholders within the firm.

Evaluation Criteria

A good product evaluation encompasses a wide variety of criteria, including market (customer), technical, and internal corporate factors. Several tests have been developed to enhance this process.

The Market Test. A fundamental question that must be answered before spending too much on developing a product idea is whether there are actually any customers willing to pay to obtain and use the proposed product.

The extent to which a market for the product may exist can be ascertained by asking some key questions, including: How important are the needs that the product would address? Do customers already perceive their need, or does the product address new needs as yet unrecognized by customers?

Eventually, the team will need to estimate how many people have the needs that are addressed by the product definition and what portion of this group (or "market share") will select this product. From these data, the potential sales volume can be estimated.

The Significant-Point-of-Difference Test. We noted in the Essential Elements section of this chapter how important it is for the new product to provide distinctive customer benefits relative to its competition. It is critical that the ways in which the product is to be superior to other alternatives be clearly defined.

The product's points of difference must be tested against the following criteria:

- Are they meaningful to customers? (That is, will the changed characteristics affect how customers will value the product?)

- Are they visible to customers? (That is, can they tell, either from viewing or using the product, that the differences are "really there"?)
- Are they positive? (That is, do they cause customers to more highly value the product?)

Fortunately, in a competitive marketplace, the products do not have to meet these criteria by a large margin. They just have to be noticeably better than the competition to induce the customer to make the choice.

The Ability to Meet the Key Challenges Test. Before deciding to develop a new product, the team needs to assess the key challenges related to developing, marketing, and using that product. How long might it take to develop the product? What are the major technical and design achievements that will be needed to make the product perform as desired? What level of innovation is needed?

Potential barriers to success are assessed here. How significantly will customers have to change their opinions or habits to use the product? What key patents held by others might prevent the team from developing the product successfully? (One significant market barrier faced by products that are sold through grocery stores, for example, is whether the product can obtain shelf space in the stores. Additionally, the product needs to be capable of withstanding the challenges presented by the characteristics of the products of key competitors.) Basically, the goal of this set of questions is to assess the major obstacles to the successful development, marketing, and use of the product and to decide whether the proposed product can surpass these challenges.

Deciding Whether or Not to Proceed

As we have shown, product ideas must be screened against quite varied factors related to customers, markets, technological progress, and the firm itself. At some point, a basis for comparison has to be established – that is, how does one decide if a product idea is "good enough" or "not good enough" to proceed? This decision is important, of course, because ideas that are approved for further development advance to the next phases in the development process and commit the company to additional investment in the idea.

Two basic approaches to deciding whether the idea (or which idea) should proceed can be taken. A common way is to evaluate each idea versus specific standards or "hurdles." For example, a firm could decide that it wants to concentrate its efforts in the small tools area and establish a minimum market share hurdle of 10 percent. Thus, an idea for a new torque wrench would be evaluated first to see if it relates to the small tools business (as the firm has defined it). Next, the wrench would be assessed to see if it had reasonable potential of capturing at least 10 percent of the torque wrench market. Each additional hurdle is evaluated, and the torque wrench idea moves to the next phase so long as the idea meets or surpasses all of the established hurdles. Both profit and market share estimates infer that the cost and price of the product are known. At this stage of development, *neither is known.* Realizing this fact, a target price and target cost should be selected. Additional cost analysis will be done later when more information is known.

An alternative approach is to evaluate ideas against each other, either one-on-one or within an overall ranking or order. Thus, the team would rank its ideas in order of "goodness" based on their overall ability to meet various criteria and select the top ideas for additional work. Both approaches have their advantages and hazards. Some of these tradeoffs are addressed in the following sections.

The Need for Multiple Criteria. In general, many criteria should be used when evaluating new product ideas. As we have suggested, the evaluation includes both qualitative and quantitative criteria. Quantitative criteria might establish minimum market size, gross margin, return on investment, or investment size limits or targets. Qualitative criteria might require products to target a specific customer group, to require no maintenance support, or to use current market channels. Market restrictions can be very important. A McKinsey study of German machine-tool makers, for example, found that the best firms developed and manufactured a narrow range of products closely related to their areas of expertise.

The overuse of a single criterion, particularly a minimum profit hurdle, can greatly distort the idea selection process. At this very early point in development, the "numbers" are gross estimates, and it likely does not make sense to eliminate an idea because its estimated return is 0.2 percent short of a 20-percent minimum hurdle rate, particularly if the idea is a base product that could spin off a number of profitable derivatives.

By just this process, IBM took itself out of the low-end copier business in 1975 at a time when it still had a chance to be competitive. A low-end product family was estimated to give a 14-percent return on investment, and the hurdle rate was 15 percent. The family of products was killed, and during the next five years other new products were defined, modeled, and killed. By 1980, no IBM low-end products had been developed, but the Japanese had more than 30 companies who had put low-end products into the marketplace during the same time period. The fundamental mistake in 1975 of assuming the calculations and estimates to be accurate within 1 percent cost IBM this business opportunity. They subsequently went out of the copier business. Ironically, the major American copier company, Xerox, was unable to produce low-end copiers during the same period for the same reason. The result was the establishment of a firm Japanese foothold in this arena.

Wheelwright and Clark (1992) suggest that firms spend too much effort on derivative products with limited potential and not enough effort on core products with large potential. A portion of the blame for this can likely be attributed to rigid hurdle processes that use too few evaluation criteria, a problem that leads to our next major point.

Variations in the Use of Criteria. The relative influences of specific criteria ought to depend on the nature of the product being evaluated – that is, there is no "one" test that can be applied to successfully evaluate all product ideas.

Many firms first sort their concepts into groups based on the characteristics of the specific project, then apply the criteria that have been decided upon for products falling within that group. Ideas are often partitioned based on the type of product (e.g., base or derivative), the anticipated total time needed to get the product to market (e.g., shorter or longer projects), and whether the product idea is within or outside of the firm's existing markets. Many different sorting factors can be used; the key is that the evaluation criteria should be customized to match the characteristics of the specific idea being evaluated.

The Need for Balance.   The idea evaluation and selection process should be balanced to avoid two undesirable extremes. Extreme #1 is a "constipated" development process where the firm cannot get product ideas through its development system and thus suffers from *too few* products. Most often, firms falling into this difficulty have unrealistic product evaluation systems that demand unobtainable performance from their new products. The key culprits are often extremely high rates of return (profit) or market shares. Since no new product can pass the unreasonable hurdles, the firm eventually finds itself with no new products.

Extreme #2 is an "overwhelmed" product development process where the firm tries to develop *too many* products. Development staff are overloaded; product introduction targets are routinely missed because projects always fall behind schedule. Once they are finally introduced, products coming out of such an overloaded process are often unreliable because key development tasks (such as product testing) have been skipped.

In this respect, the rank/order selection method can be used effectively to avoid these two extremes. Because most firms have limited development resources, it is possible that a company may have more good ideas than it has the resources to develop at once. Using the rank/order method, the firm can fund its "best" product ideas down to the point at which its development resources are committed.

Product Ideas

When Ideas "Fail."   Those ideas that do not pass muster should be documented and saved. In particular, the reasons why the idea was rejected should be noted; as circumstances change, an idea that was originally rejected may become a good idea sometime in the future. For example, an idea rejected at one point because no technologies yet exist to deliver the required level of performance may become viable as new technologies are developed. As such, previously rejected ideas should be reviewed occasionally.

The Enhanced Product Concept Description.   The contents of the initial Product Concept Description should be updated to reflect the team's current thinking about what the product should be, based on their information gathering and screening activities. As a test of completeness, the team can evaluate its enhanced Product Concept Description by reconsidering how well the description answers clearly the previous set of four questions used at the initial idea stage:

- What are the product's essential features and functions?
- Who are the product's customers and what are their applications?
- What are the product's essential benefits to the customers?
- When is the product needed?

The description is checked to ensure that it clearly defines *the product's essential benefits to the customer.* Why will customers value the product? What makes this product different and better than other potential alternatives that are available, including directly competing products, the use of fundamentally different methods or equipment, or choosing to do without?

The *target customer(s)* should be explicitly defined as well. What are the key characteristics or features of this product's target customer? If the user and the buyer of the product are not the same person, these differences are defined. The Product Concept Description may also explain how (and how easily) use of the product will mesh with the customers' normal routines or procedures.

Summary

As ideas are evaluated and the best ones are selected for additional development, the team compiles its results into a Product Concept Description, which is the major output of the Product Ideas phase.

The Product Concept Description should not be a detailed specification. It should instead be a one- or two-page summary that captures the key highlights of the proposed product. It can be written as several short paragraphs, or – even better – as a bulleted outline. It is often useful to write the description as if it were a customer pamphlet or brochure; this approach will help the team to keep its focus on the customer's viewpoint.

The Product Concept Description serves three major purposes: to summarize the critical results from the concept screening process, to define the major benefits to be provided by the new product, and to summarize the key knowledge or assumptions upon which the concept was approved for additional development.

References

Duerr, Michael G. (1986), *The Commercial Development of New Products*, The Conference Board, Washington, DC.

Selected Bibliography

Kuczmarski, Thomas D. (1988), *Managing New Products: Competing Through Excellence*, Prentice Hall, Englewood Cliffs, NJ.

Wheelwright, Steven C., and Kim B. Clark (1992), *Revolutionizing Product Development: Quantum Leaps in Speed, Efficiency, and Quality*, The Free Press, New York.

CHAPTER 4

CUSTOMER FUTURE NEEDS PROJECTION

Many large US firms have been playing catch-up to foreign competition since the 1970s and 1980s, when they learned that customer brand loyalty alone could not compete against the nearly error-free products from Japanese firms. Their immediate reaction was to undertake an enormous competitive product analysis to learn why competitors' products were superior. Following that effort were competitive analyses of firms' manufacturing and product development processes to determine why competitive products could be sold at lower prices and how they could be developed so rapidly. The term "benchmarking" became a household word throughout business literature.

We highlight the projection of *future* needs to prevent an overemphasis on benchmarking efforts, while at the same time recognizing that benchmarking is an essential method for assessing competitiveness in one's products and processes. *The limiting feature of benchmarking is that it, alone, is not enough.* The firm that designs a new product to meet requirements determined from benchmarking alone will assure itself of being at least one product cycle behind. (Of course, this is better than being two or more design cycles behind!) We emphasize the concept of projecting customers' future needs so that the firm's next generation of products will be competitive when they are launched. The Customer Future Needs Projection phase is highlighted in figure 4.1.

Milestone Goals

The milestone goals for the Customer Future Needs Projection phase are *to define the product's target customers and to project their future needs*. A new product must solve customers' needs during its entire market life, which, of course, is in the future,

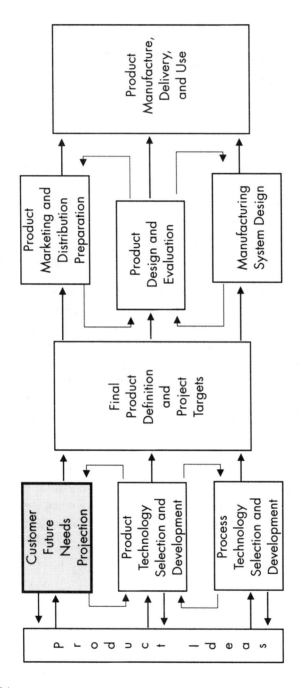

Figure 4.1. The Customer Future Needs Projection phase within the overall product development process.

because the new product does not yet exist. Thus, the new product must address future customer needs, not merely current ones. Competitive benchmarking is performed to understand competitors' products and capabilities so that the new product can be superior to competitive offerings.

During the Customer Future Needs Projection phase, the team strives to project customers' future needs so that the new product can be specified to meet them when the product is developed and ready for sale.

Figure 4.2 illustrates the crucial need for projecting needs forward in time. The lower left-hand corner of the figure, labeled "Now," illustrates a situation where benchmarking studies show a relatively small gap between one's product and its competition. One could erroneously conclude that the new product only needs to be slightly improved over today's product. However, if one considers that competitors are also developing improved products, then one's product goals must be significantly higher if that product is to be truly "ahead" once it finally becomes available for sale (at the "first customer ship" date). Additionally, the figure shows that as the new product reaches the end of its market life new competitive products eventually pass it. Thus, one always needs a next generation of follow-on products to stay ahead. The graph clearly shows the need for continual improvement of one's product line.

Many firms are reluctant to invest in products that make their present product line obsolete, even though history repeatedly demonstrates that if you don't make your own products obsolete with new products, your competition will! Firms that wait are repeatedly behind and must make a mighty effort once they realize that they have lost significant ground. The engineering and manufacturing groups in these organizations are forced to react continually to competitive moves – a very stressful and ineffective mode in which to operate over many years.

Process Description

In the just-completed Product Ideas phase, the team took a brief look at the product's potential customers, marketplace, and

56

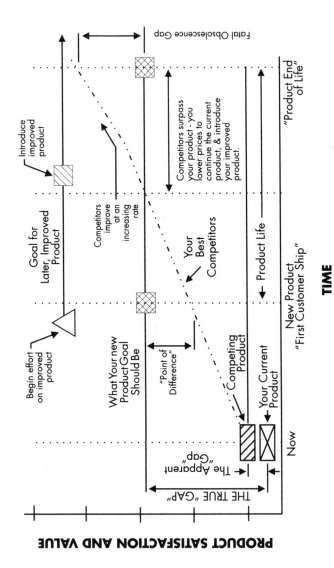

Figure 4.2. Projecting product requirements based on future needs.

competitors. In the Customer Future Needs Projection phase, a more-comprehensive assessment is undertaken. Competing products and processes are benchmarked and customer needs investigated thoroughly, to gain a comprehensive understanding of what the product must be and do to be successful. Needs are defined and checked in terms of future needs and ranked in order of importance. Finally, assumptions and estimates in the Product Concept Description are confirmed, modified, and/or disproved. These activities all fall under the topics for the Customer Future Needs Projection phase shown in figure 4.3.

Essential Elements

The essential elements for the Customer Future Needs Projection phase steer the team toward developing an in-depth understanding of both the customer needs and the competition. These elements are:

- A study of product use in the customer environment and the identification of new needs for the product based on this information;
- A customer definition of quality;
- Competitive analysis (benchmarking); and
- The participation of experienced and creative design engineers in the product benchmarking and customer needs investigations.

A Study of Product Use in the Customer Environment

The most competitive firms make a large effort to discover the future needs of the customer in the early stage of development (i.e., in this phase). They investigate these needs with more than just focus group interviews or surveys, although these focus interviews are valuable. They actually send their senior technical people into the customer environment to see what current needs are and to project them based upon the actual work to be done.

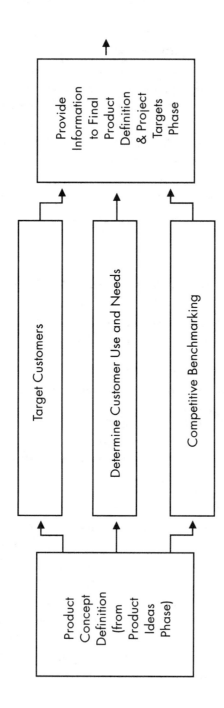

Figure 4.3. The Customer Future Needs Projection phase.

A Customer Definition of Quality

A comprehensive understanding of the customers' quality perceptions and expectations is essential if the team is to develop a product design that meets or exceeds those expectations. As demonstrated in chapter 2, these expectations can be assessed using widely differing techniques. The team that developed the force-deflection measure for assessing keyboard touch certainly needed a different approach than did the inkjet printer team that was trying to assess print quality. Nonetheless, the purpose of both efforts was to capture the customers' expectations for the product's quality.

A Competitive Analysis (Benchmarking)

The technique of effective competitive analysis is an essential element for assessing the customers' current product alternatives. The goal of this effort is to provide the team with a fundamental understanding of competing products and their best features, and likely product trends (i.e., new standards or areas of major improvement). The most effective teams assess not only competitors' products, product substitutes, and industry trends, but also evaluate their product development capabilities, manufacturing ability, costs, and speed.

This benchmarking of other firms' technologies, design practices, manufacturing processes, materials, and other factors establish the standards by which the product development effort should be judged. The best benchmarking efforts compare the firm's operations to those of the world's best competitors, regardless of their industry. Thus a computer manufacturer might benchmark itself by comparing its product ordering and delivery capabilities against those of a mail-order catalog firm that is well known for its superior ordering services. A more detailed discussion of benchmarking will be presented later.

The Participation of Experienced and Creative Design Engineers

This essential element can be satisfied only if a firm's management realizes that the participation of key technical people who are in direct contact with customers is not a waste of time.

Within functionally based product development organizations, customer contacts are typically made by a product planning or marketing group. Yet having experienced and creative design engineers participate directly in these investigations dramatically increases the probability of developing innovative solutions to customer needs. In particular, the development team's ability to project future customer needs increases from these contacts. A creative design engineer who sees a customer need firsthand often becomes highly motivated to develop an innovative solution to that need. This kind of information is a much more powerful motivator than a needs list arising from a product marketing group.

Customers and Their Needs

Target Customers

In the Product Concept Description, the team began to define the identity of target customers and their needs. In this phase, a more comprehensive understanding is developed.

Customer Identification. The first step in the process is to identify the target customers and users for the product. This issue needs to be addressed from several viewpoints: Whom does the product serve or benefit? Who are the users? Who are the buyers?

The most obvious customers of a product are its actual users, but a supporting cast of other customers may exist as well. Software-intensive products, in particular, are likely to have a variety of secondary customers. Consider that:

- A product installer may need to adjust system options to tailor the product for a specific use;
- A system administrator may need to restrict access to certain product options, set user access privileges, set usage limits, and the like; and
- A system monitor for the product may be assigned to provide supporting services for other users, such as scheduling, data backup or recovery, or auxiliary data linkage.

Another key question is whether the customer is also the person or persons who actually purchase the product. If the product is to be sold to organizations like large firms, the needs of several very different people may influence the purchase decision. The requirements of the purchasing agent, the manufacturing manager, and the machine operator may differ greatly, but if they affect the decision as to whether or not a product is purchased, they all need to be met if the product is to be successful. All people in these categories should be identified if they have any effect on the purchase and use of the product.

The manufacturing and service functions within the organization must also be viewed as customers. Having design engineers tour the existing manufacturing processes for a predecessor or similar product encourages powerful input, as it gives designers the chance to hear firsthand from the manufacturing people what problems exist and suggestions for product improvement. In addition, to have design engineers spend a day servicing the product with the service organization generates more powerful input. Putting firsthand experiences together with written input from these "customers" provides the needed incentive and information for design engineers to solve problems of which they might otherwise be unaware.

Customer Profile.   Once the various customers have been identified, the next task is to develop a better understanding of each of these customer groups by creating profiles of them. The basic question is "What are the traits of these customers?"

A good way to get started is to assess the general nature or culture of the customers. Are they slow-paced and deliberate, or fast-paced and innovative? How do they react to change? What level of resources (e.g., cash or assets) do they have? Are the customers willing to assume financial risk?

The level and types of technical skills held by users affect whether the product is used successfully, so these should be investigated. Users may be categorized not only in terms of their job function (i.e., installers, operators, administrators, end users) but also by their product knowledge and skills. If different classes of users exist (e.g., beginners versus experienced, general purpose versus special skill), the product might be designed so that it can accommodate these differences. The Apple Macintosh, for example, has a context-sensitive user "balloon help" feature that can be turned on for new users or disabled for experienced users. Understanding the relative distribution of these skills among customers can greatly affect the product requirements.

Customers of a given product generally share a set of common characteristics, related either directly or indirectly to the needs that the product is designed to satisfy. By identifying these common traits, the team can adapt the product's definition and its marketing to more closely match those traits. Concentrations may be geographic ("southeastern US," "city dwellers"), industrial ("machine shops"), demographic ("women over 40"), or common customer interests ("avid bicyclists"). The characteristics of the firm's current customers can be compared to those for the proposed product to evaluate how well knowledge of the firm's current customers can be used in developing this product.

A customer profile provides the needed perspective for deciding the importance of various user functions. Software products and products utilizing software for control are particularly vulnerable to being loaded down with requirements of questionable value. The better the understanding of the customer's characteristics and needs, the better the basis for setting priorities among product functions and allocating resources according those needs.

Customer Needs

As repeatedly suggested, products exist to address customer needs. Obviously, then, a better understanding of those needs ought to lead to a product that better addresses those needs. Superior teams spend significant time investigating both *what* problem is to be solved and *why* it needs solving. They also look for relationships between the direct needs expressed by customers and other, more-fundamental needs.

The Identification of Important Factors. Customers look for solutions with the best combination of such things as specific functions or performance, cost savings, convenience, ease of use, time savings, reliability, and dozens of other factors. The specific combination of these factors can vary greatly, not only among different customers but also with the same customer over time.

Since the development goal is to create a product with maximum customer value, the team investigates how customers assign value to the product's benefits. What benefits do customers want most from the product? What new benefits are needed? Do they compute cost savings versus use of other products, compare certain specifications, or use more esoteric criteria? If customer value and quality perceptions can be measured, development work on these measurements begins now. The team also begins to compile information on other major factors that will influence the product's use. Examples of these factors include the need to meet certain safety regulations, interface needs to other equipment, and other restrictions.

Need Awareness and Occurrence. The team also has to determine when these customer needs occur. Does the need for the product exist now, or does the product address some anticipated future need? What events or situations create the customers' need for the product? When and how often do these events occur?

In terms of the marketing and market life of the product, the team also assesses whether customers already sense the need for the product and how long the identified need will continue to exist.

Understanding Real Needs. A key objective for the Customer Future Needs Projection phase is to find customers' real needs and to identify innovative ways for potentially satisfying them. The difficulty with this seemingly simple concept is that customers tend to express their needs in terms of their past or current experience, so that underlying needs are not always readily apparent. Additionally, customers do not always express what is most important to them. Although rental car customers talk most about not wanting to wait in line, one researcher found that it was the rental car's dependability that was much more important in determining customer satisfaction [Levine, 1990, p.106]. Traditional market analyses often fail to reveal this real context behind customers' expressed needs. Some of the so-called "customer-driven" or "market-driven" initiatives that are so highly touted by many companies fall into this trap as well.

The key to understanding underlying customer needs is to discover what the product really means to its customers and users. A fax machine is not just a combination scanner-printer; what it really means to customers is that they can "make documents travel fast." Printer users may say they want a print resolution of 600 dots per inch, but their underlying need may simply be a way to make diagonal lines appear less jagged. By blindly accepting customers' expressed needs, the team loses an opportunity to satisfy the real need in other ways, such as by using software "line-blending" techniques.

Superior new products "leap" to exceptional benefits by challenging the basic assumptions of existing products. A simplified example illustrates this "leaping" concept. Early this century, families who wanted to keep items frozen purchased ice from suppliers, who then delivered the ice to the home. If asked what their needs were, these customers might have said, "We need more frequent ice deliveries." The obvious solution, of course, is to increase delivery frequency, at an obvious increase in cost. A more-thorough assessment of the expressed need might have revealed the "real" customer desire – to keep items frozen at all times. Once the real need is understood, the innovative firm can pursue a leaping solution and begin development of products to keep things frozen longer, such as better insulated containers and the electric freezer. The firm thus challenges two key assumptions of that time: that ice at home cannot be kept frozen longer and that ice cannot be made at home.

Change in Needs over Time. The relative importance of performance parameters continually changes over time. Thus, a key question to be answered is "Which needs are becoming more important to customers?"

When first introduced, new capabilities add "excitement" to

the product; customers are delighted that the product can now accomplish something that it once did not. But over time, customers become so accustomed to the "excitement" feature that it changes into an "expected" one; customers then expect any product they choose in that category to meet that minimum capability.

Knowing which product capabilities are expected and which are exciting is important because they have different effects on customer value perceptions. The inclusion of exciting features can provide the significant point of difference that the product needs – the extra customer value that makes it superior to other alternatives. On the other hand, the failure to provide an expected capability can cause customers to reject the product simply because it fails to meet a customer-defined minimum standard. The minimum customer needs investigation, therefore, needs to at least capture these minimum requirements, since neglecting to include these in the new product dooms that product to failure.

We discussed the necessity to project customer needs into the future, so we will not repeat those considerations here. However, it is important for the team to assess in what ways and how fast these customer needs may change throughout the product's market life.

Customer Comprehension of Radical Alternatives. The literature is full of cases where market research has failed to predict accurately the success or failure of a radically new product. IBM's initial study of the potential mainframe computer market in the 1950s suggested that they might be able to sell just a few units. Early market studies of copiers concluded that customers preferred carbon paper. The 3M post-it note even failed several marketing tests before eventually becoming successful. Thus, the team should take extraordinary care when assessing the customer needs and potential benefits concerning a new product that is substantially different from existing products.

Methods for Assessment. The importance of understanding customer needs naturally leads to the question, "What methods can be used to determine these needs?" *In general, we have found no substitute for repeated, direct contact with customers by the members of the development team.* To structure these contacts, the case study teams successfully used many of the traditional market research techniques, subject to the limitations that we have noted previously. Focus-group-type activities appear to be increasingly used for extracting underlying needs from customers.

Specific aspects of the product can be evaluated now as well. User interfaces for the product can be tested quite early using either hardware and software models. Different physical control layouts can be evaluated by users to find the most useful and ergonomic configurations. If the product has a software-driven interface, early prototypes of information display screens can help customers to express their information and display needs. Customers will often react more accurately to a specific stimulus than they can to an abstract question about the same subject.

Product benchmarking can be used to identify the key disadvantages of current products and to generate ideas on how best to prevent the problems with current products that displease customers. Customers who agree to assist the team can review proposed product specifications and test early prototype units of the product.

Understanding Current Capabilities – Competitive Benchmarking

The importance of undertaking an effective competitive analysis was emphasized earlier as an essential element for the Customer Future Needs Projection phase. Xerox, Motorola, and other award-winning firms have promoted the term "competitive benchmarking" to describe this "process of measuring (one's) products, services, and practices against (its) toughest competitors, or those recognized as world leaders" [Xerox, 1989, p.4]. By including the "practices" of competitors, the best firms extend their analyses beyond competitors' products to include their competitive capabilities as well, in the following list. Benchmarking is performed to identify industry cost and performance standards in these areas and how those standards might be achieved or exceeded [Hadden, 1986, p.11].

The steps in competitive benchmarking are

- Identifying the competing firms,
- Identifying the competing products,
- Benchmarking the product,
- Benchmarking the market, and
- Benchmarking the business and processes.

Identifying Competitors

A fairly obvious step within any benchmarking effort is to identify the firm's key competitors: How many firms compete in this product area? Who are they? Given the increasingly global nature of competition, both national and foreign firms are investigated. When considering the development of a new base product (and particularly a new breakthrough product), the potential for new entrants has to be considered. What other firms might also be pursuing the development of a similar product now, or would be as soon as they became aware of this new product?

The competitive strengths and weaknesses of key competitors are assessed to look for potential barriers to success and to identify opportunities. What proprietary technologies, patents, or technical skills are held by other firms that will make them difficult to compete against?

Identifying Competitive Products

Products that are expected to compete directly against the proposed product also need to be identified. Both domestic and foreign products should be considered. While currently available products are much more obvious and much easier to assess, the team should also consider what new products will arise during the new product's life.

Gaining a complete understanding of the product's competition requires that the team also identify which substitute products compete against the proposed product. Customers generally have multiple alternatives when faced with a task, so that any product that performs that task also competes against these alternatives, including the option to *not* do the task. Because value is dependent on both performance and price, a full range of product substitutes – those that perform well and are more expensive and those that perform less well and are less expensive – should be analyzed.

As an example, Hewlett-Packard laser printers compete not only against Lexmark International laser printers but also against dot-matrix printers and bubble-jet printers. In some applications, they even compete against pen plotters. Thus, when assessing its potential value, a new printer product needs to be compared to all of these alternatives.

Product (or Technical) Benchmarking

Once appropriate competitive products are identified, they are compared to the proposed product. How do features, performance, and other customer-identified features of the proposed product compare to these alternatives? Both market information (such as competitor's marketing brochures) and physical product testing are important sources of information about competitive offerings. Often, these results can be compiled into a cross-reference table for simpler analysis.

A historical assessment of competing products can help the team to identify major new product trends. When compared to products of several product generations ago, in what ways are new competing products providing increased value to customers? How have technologies, features, speed, and so forth changed from the older products to the newer products? At what rate have manufacturing costs changed?

Another useful technique is to disassemble and "reverse engineer" competitive products to understand how they operate, what technologies they employ, and what materials they use. The manufacturing cost of the product can often be estimated quite accurately this way.

Market Benchmarking

This topic encompasses a wide array of issues related to the environment in which the new product is to be sold. Competing products and the firms that sell them are evaluated on issues such as their market shares, pricing strategies with recent products, and rate of new product introductions. New base product development efforts may want to compare the firm's projected product mix to those expected to be offered by competitors.

How the products are sold is important to their success; thus, the number and size of distribution channels used to market and sell the products often need to be assessed. Marketing and advertising spending (on a total, per-product, and/or per-unit basis) and relative brand name recognition may also need analysis, particularly if building customer awareness of the product is likely to be a problem.

Some general judgments that may be reached using market benchmarking include conclusions about what major differences exist between the successful and unsuccessful products within this category, the general extent of competition for this product (fiercely competitive? limited?), and the public's perception of the reputation and strengths of the various competitors (e.g., "leader in printers," "technically innovative," or "low-cost alternative"). A key conclusion for many efforts is to identify the gaps in existing competitive product lines that may represent a market opportunity for the new product.

Business and Processes Benchmarking

In chapter 1, we showed how process benchmarking enabled Xerox to discover its product development deficiencies. This type of benchmarking is increasingly used because it provides a structured, formalized method for comparing the practices of the firm with those of other firms.

Of the two, business benchmarking is more common, perhaps because the information is more easily obtained (at least for publicly traded firms). Typical business comparisons to competitors are made with respect to financial performance indicators such as net sales, operating profit, return on assets, and other financial ratios. Relative debt levels and cash availability can also be reviewed to evaluate the financial ability of the firm to develop new products. The organizational structure of the firm may also be compared to those of its competitors to evaluate their relative strengths.

While business benchmarking tends to measure the "ends" (the results of the firm's efforts), process benchmarking measures the "means" (how the firms perform those efforts). Process benchmarking compares the firm to its competitors with respect to critical abilities such as its product development processes, technology management and use skills, and manufacturing capabilities. In this respect, process benchmarking is the critical enabler, because its results show how a given performance was actually attained. Firms limiting themselves to business benchmarking may recognize a weakness, but generally will not be able to ascertain the cause of that weakness without performing the corresponding process benchmarking.

The relative ability of a firm to develop new products can be measured quantitatively through an assortment of parameters, including the number of new products developed per time period, the number of product development engineers, and the amount of time needed to develop new products. Other parameters, such as R&D spending and average hours worked, can also be useful. Qualitative product development comparisons can be made relative to what development phases are used, whether a single team leader is used, and so on. Design practices can be assessed relative to such items as the number of parts used in comparable products, the relative ease of manufacture, and the use of innovative design concepts.

A company's technological acumen can be assessed by evaluating factors such as the number of new technologies developed by a firm over time, the number of patents (total and per employee), and how new technologies have been incorporated in the firm's new products. The use of various technologies to accomplish specific tasks can also be compared: When function x is needed, what technologies are used by that firm to accomplish it?

Standard benchmarks of a company's manufacturing capability include basic measures such as total manufacturing capacity, investment, and cost structure. In the cost category, output per employee, overhead costs, the time required to build an equivalent product (i.e., the cycle time), and the existence (or lack) of economies of scale in production can be analyzed. Manufacturing quality can be estimated by evaluating the product's early customer failure rate and reviewing the firm's quality management approach. Since purchased materials comprise a large portion of total manufacturing cost, material purchasing policies are often worthy of investigation. What percentage of the product's parts are purchased rather than made? How is each firm's purchasing organized, and how constructive are its relations with suppliers? How many purchasing specialists does the firm have and how long does it take to complete a purchase order?

Relative manufacturing capabilities can also be reviewed to identify needed improvements in production skills and management. What manufacturing processes are used by competitors, and how effectively? What special skills do they have? How are competitors' production processes organized? Which use self-contained manufacturing teams? In what ways are these organizations more effective?

The most successful firms benchmark their most critical activities, or processes, against not only their direct competitors, but also against firms from any industries that perform those processes best. For example, if the firm has identified "fast product delivery" as a critical process, then it will want to identify potential benchmarks to measure that process. In this case, potential measures might include the percentage of deliveries completed in less than one day, the number of delivery errors per week, and the percentage of lost shipments. In addition to benchmarking against its direct competitors, the firm also might choose to benchmark other firms that are well known for fast delivery, such as Federal Express or Domino's Pizza. The key is to identify the firms that perform these essential processes best, create methods for measuring the quality of these processes, and use the benchmarks for finding ways to improve process performance.

Cautions

Even with this fairly lengthy discussion, only a small number of the potential benchmarks that can be used to compare a firm to its competitors have been mentioned. Clearly, then, benchmarking can be a major activity requiring significant effort and resources to accomplish. Also, benchmarking measures the current capabilities of competitors, not their future ones. Therefore, capabilities and needs must also be projected into the future.

Some firms have overcome this problem by making their benchmarking activities a more continuous process. In this way, firms can more easily observe trends and can build their information gradually over time. Xerox, for example, started with about a dozen benchmarking measures, but over ten years that number has grown to more than 200 [Xerox, 1989, p.4]. New product teams can use the benchmarking results from previous teams to get a head start and to minimize the new effort required to gain a comprehensive understanding of the competitive environment.

Other Customer Considerations

Customer Acceptance Issues

Another major area for investigation is to look for any major customer use or acceptance barriers that might impair the product's success. The new product might cause the customer's existing equipment to be incompatible or useless, which could make customers reluctant to change. The team may find that customers historically have been very sensitive to product price. Government regulations or fear of liability might limit customer flexibility for trying the new approaches presented in the new product.

Particular attention should be paid to how much customers will have to alter their operations or habits to use the product effectively, particularly if the target customer group tends to prefer stability over change. What changes in equipment, operating procedures, or staff will customers have to make in order to use the product? Along this line, the team should assess whether the customer will be able use the product immediately or will need training. Operator and maintenance training can become a substantial investment for many products.

Once these potential barriers are identified, the team can

work to eliminate or overcome them, either through how the product is marketed or in the specification or design of the product itself. For example, the team might consider providing a certain amount of on-site operator training along with the product. Or perhaps the operating controls of the product can be designed to reduce training requirements.

Ranking Needs

The tremendous number of customer needs and considerations that must be evaluated to complete a comprehensive customer needs assessment can be overwhelming to the development team. If the technical challenge of designing a product to meet all of these needs is added, the development task becomes truly daunting, if not outright impossible.

A common but most ineffective method for defining the customer needs for a new product is to compile a laundry list that details every feature and performance element of every competing product, then demands that the new product exceed all of the items on the list. The overall size of the resulting demand list and the inevitable technical conflicts that arise among the various needs make this a totally unworkable approach. Yet, in functional organizations where the marketing function provides requirements to the design function, this process is often attempted. The resulting contention between the functional groups can greatly delay the product's development.

Instead, customer needs need to be prioritized or ranked based on the team's evaluation of how they affect customer perceptions of the product's value. In some circumstances, this means that some less important current market requirements must be ignored so that the team can pursue the significant product improvements that are needed to meet future needs. We have found Middendorf's [1986] three-tier ranking of goals (requirement, goal, preference) to be a simple but useful start for ranking customer needs.

An "operational usage profile" should also be developed to estimate how frequently product functions will actually be used [Musa, 1993; Whittaker and Poore, 1993]. Frequently used functions need to be distinguished from the product's "bells and whistles" so that the product definition and development activities prioritize the most frequently used functions. The usage profile is particularly important for software functions, because the intangible nature of software can lead to the creation of an unrealistically long software requirements list. When this oversized requirements list is pruned to match the proposed software development schedule, knowledge of how often product functions are likely to be used by customers enables the team to make customer-oriented decisions.

Interaction with Technology Selection and Development Activities

A commonly underused function of the customer needs effort is to ascertain customer preferences regarding critical technical tradeoffs that may have to be made so that the product can be designed. For example, a technology may be capable of operating at a faster speed, but only at the sacrifice of its usable life. At some point during product development, engineers will need guidance as to where to set that speed – faster for more performance or slower for longer life? The basis for making the best decision is to determine what combination of speed versus life will best meet customer needs, but this can only be known if the issue has been investigated. Thus, the technology staff and the needs investigation members must communicate which potential tradeoffs apply (and *how* they apply) so that customer needs can be properly assessed.

In the other direction, technology advances can be evaluated for their potential of improving customer use, operation, quality, or other benefits of the product. Many products are just now, for example, harnessing advanced computing technologies in "smart machines" (machines with embedded microcontrollers) and in the interactive systems of these machines. The increasing capacity and decreasing cost of computer memory enable more powerful information storage, retrieval, control, and display, even in small, portable devices. Fiber-optic networks, wireless communications, speech and handwriting recognition, and other advanced technologies are eliminating constraints with regard to how products and users interact.

Summary

Selecting the proper combination of product features, performance, and other product benefits to meet customers' future needs is an exceedingly difficult task. The features and functions that are most critical to customers must be identified and the product characterized in terms of an appropriate combination of highest performance, lowest cost, and the fastest possible development time. The team must exercise careful judgment while assessing the product design tradeoffs that are involved.

The output of this phase may include a revision of the Product Concept Document. This refinement may occur as the project emerges from the Customer Future Needs Projection phase. It is a revised statement of the new product's function, customers, and benefits, based on new information about customer expectations and competitive benchmarks. Other outputs include documents that describe all of the benchmarking activities. Most importantly, a list of product needs (prioritized as requirement, goal, or preference) will accompany the Product Concept Document. This significant information and conclusions regarding customer needs, product markets, pricing, and other considerations are collected, organized, and made available for use during the next phase – the Final Product Definition and Project Targets phase.

References

Hadden, L. L. (1986), "Product Development at Xerox: Meeting the Competitive Challenge," notes from presentation to Copying and Duplicating Industry Conference, February 10 – 12, 1986.

Levine, Joshua (1990), "How'm I Doin'?" *Forbes*, December 24, 1990, pp. 106 – 9.

Middendorf, William H. (1990), *Design of Devices and Systems*, Marcel Dekker, New York.

Musa, John D. (1993), "Operational Profiles in Software-Reliability Engineering," *IEEE Software*, March 1993, pp. 14 – 32.

Whittaker, J. W. and J. H. Poore (1993), "Markov Analysis of Software Specifications," *ACM Transactions on Software Engineering and Methodology*, January 1993, pp. 93 – 106.

Xerox Corporation (1989), *National Quality Award Application Abstract*, an abstract of Xerox's application for the 1989 Malcolm Baldrige National Quality Award, Xerox Corporation, Rochester, NY.

CHAPTER 5

TECHNOLOGY SELECTION AND DEVELOPMENT

The competitive need to shorten development cycle time makes the Technology Selection and Development phases (highlighted in figure 5.1) critical to the timely development of superior quality products. This chapter identifies these essential elements for product technology selection and development that allow the project to be planned and executed with the appropriate emphasis on technology *selection, development, and verification.*

Since they occur very early in the product development process, the Technology Selection and Development phases have a significant impact on the outcome of the product development process. Product and process technologies are combined with customer needs information to establish the product definition. These key technologies are the basis for product design and manufacturing system design. The proper selection and development of product and process technologies are imperative to the development of a superior, technologically innovative product.

Milestone Goals

The milestone goals for the Technology Selection and Development phases are *to choose appropriate, affordable, robust technologies for products and processes, and to pass the Technical Feasibility Phase Review.*

Properly selected product technologies meet customers' value expectations, work properly in a product environment, and are manufacturable with high yields. Properly selected process technologies are controllable and capable of producing high-quality products economically. A robust product technology performs as intended even when subjected to

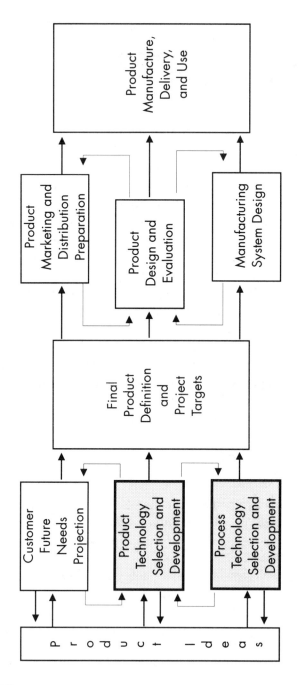

Figure 5.1. The Product Technology Selection and Development phases (product and process) within the overall product development process.

operational and environmental variations, manufacturing or process tolerances, and other unfavorable conditions. Significant parameters affecting the performance of the technology must be understood during design and controlled during production.

Robust, appropriate, and affordable technologies meet the product requirements at an affordable cost, as stated in a Technology Feasibility Statement. Since the choice of an appropriate technology is critically important, the first major management review of the development effort (called a "phase gate" by some firms) is often a Technical Feasibility Phase Review.

Process Description

The Technology Selection and Development Phase of the product development process is comprised of four basic tasks: evaluation of technology alternatives, technology selection, technology development, and technology verification as shown in Figure 5.2. The Customer Future Needs Projection phase steers the team toward developing an in-depth understanding of both the customer needs and the competition (see figure 5.2). The time and effort required to complete this phase are significantly different depending on whether an existing or a new (i.e., undeveloped) technology is selected.

Figure 5.2 also indicates that the initial technology evaluation generally encompasses both existing and new technologies. All technology candidates are evaluated for a limited time, after which the most promising one is selected for additional development and verification. If a new technology is selected, it must be developed during the New Technology Development step. Finally, the selected technology's ability (either existing or new) to meet the proposed product requirements is verified during the Technology Feasibility Verification.

Essential Elements

The essential elements for the Technology Selection and Development phases are:

- Technology evaluation
  - The discovery of critical variables;
  - The demonstration of an operating space; and
  - The discovery of inherent technology limitations.
- Technology selection
  - Customer criteria used in selection;
  - Early selection;
  - The consideration of several candidates; and
  - New versus existing technology considerations.
- Technology development
  - The optimization of the operating space;
  - Variability minimization; and
  - Simultaneous product and process technology development.
- Technology feasibility verification
  - Critical variables defined, quantified, and targeted;
  - Critical requirements demonstrated; and
  - The drafting of a Technology Feasibility Statement.

Note the correspondence of the four groups of elements to the four stages of evaluation, selection, development, and verification. The Essential Elements are designed to ensure the selection and development of robust technologies and to avoid the choice of fragile technologies.

Ensuring a Correct Technology Choice through the Essential Elements

The Consequences of a Fragile Technology

Severe product quality problems and development schedule delays may be created if a machine is designed using a "fragile" technology – a technology that is not under control or that is not understood adequately. Although in today's environment short development schedules are a very high priority, rushed technology selections, made before the technology is well understood, often set the stage for spectacular design failures, perplexing manufacturing problems, and lengthy development delays.

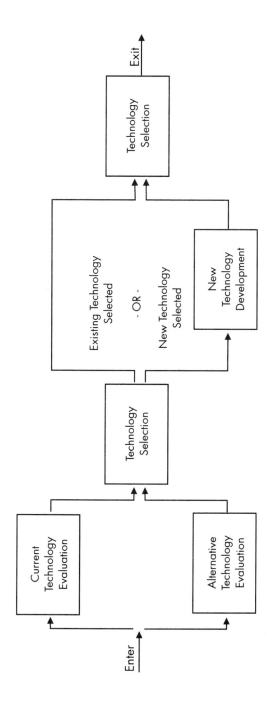

Figure 5.2. Technology Selection and Development phase for an innovative product.

81

The consequence of rushing a fragile technology into a product design is well illustrated by an effort to accelerate the development and manufacture of new-technology, composite wings for a military aircraft. The new composite technology was rushed into the design phase. Then, with the design 40 percent complete, the first wing model ripped apart in a wind-tunnel test. To correct the design, plastic sheets were added to the composite. Then assembly workers found they could not attach the wing parts together because the new plastic layers separated around the bolted connections. To fix this problem, special shims were designed and rushed into the manufacturing process. After 29,000 bolts were installed, engineers discovered that the new shims made the bolts too short. All 29,000 bolts had to be inspected and 4,000 replaced. One development manager summarized the effort: "We took shortcuts trying to meet the schedule, and we failed. We were trying to do things so fast that we ended up shooting ourselves in the foot as we walked along." In the end, the new wing cost twice as much as its "current technology" counterpart and was delivered significantly behind schedule [Carley, 1989].

While proper technology selection and development can significantly improve the quality and pace of product development, poor technology selections and inadequate technology development can lead to lengthy project delays, large development cost overruns, and/or project failure.

Definitions of Critical Variables and Operating Space

Before the essential elements are discussed in more detail, some definitions of recurring terms are needed.

Critical variables determine the output of a technology. For example, the critical variables that determine how well the toner is fixed to the paper in the hot roll fuser of a copier or laser printer are temperature, pressure, and time. A combination of values for these three variables determines whether satisfactory attachment or fixing of the toner to the paper occurs.

The throughput capacity for a product with embedded software may depend on memory and microprocessor speed. In a laser printer, for example, processing time will vary for pages of varying complexity. A page is processed in chunks, and the upper limit on chunk size is determined by memory. Similarly, the rate at which chunks are moved through processing steps is determined by the speed of the microprocessor. Memory and microprocessor speed, therefore, are also critical variables in laser printers.

The *operating space* for a technology is the range of critical variables over which the output from the technology meets requirements. In the hot roll fuser example given earlier, the range of temperature, pressure, and time over which the toner is adequately fixed to the paper creates an operating space of the critical variables for the fuser. The fuser is set to operate in an operating space box surrounded by a safety factor region (see figure 5.3). This margin allows the fuser to operate acceptably even if some unusual event (such as a temperature measurement shift) should cause the fuser to operate outside its normal temperature range. The quantified measures developed for assessing the fusing quality of the toner are used later during the Product Design and Evaluation phase to assess the evolving product's ability to meet the Product Design Specification. With these definitions in mind, the essential elements can be discussed.

Technology Evaluation

Three common factors, derived from the case studies, apply to all evaluation activity throughout the Technology Selection and Development phase. These three essential elements also help to integrate all technology evaluation activity into a focused and coherent effort. These elements are:

- The discovery of critical variables;
- The demonstration of an operating space; and
- The discovery of inherent technology limitations.

The Discovery of Critical Variables. The first essential element is to discover the critical variables that determine or control the output of the technology. This element is especially important when contemplating selection of a new technology, since few facts are available with which to perform an evaluation

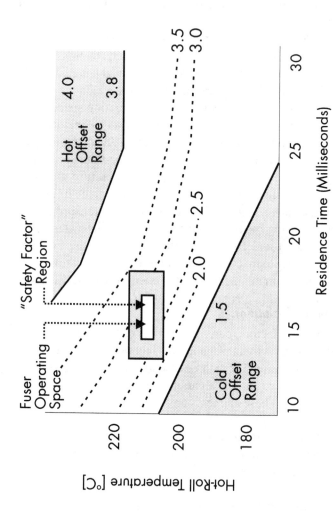

Figure 5.3. An example of an operating space. (Redrawn from Wilson, 1979. Used by permission.)

[Voit, 1988]. Both analysis and experimentation are useful to determine those factors that are critical to the desired operation of the technology.

The Demonstration of an Operating Space. Once the critical controlling variables are discovered, an operating space for the critical variables of the technology must be demonstrated. The technology team must be able to project that an adequate operating space for the critical variables can be developed *before starting the product design* – otherwise, the technology must be rejected as too fragile. The product and process design have to be capable of controlling all critical variables within the technology's operating space. Statistically designed experiments are particularly valuable in quantifying the location and size of the operating space.

The Discovery of Inherent Technology Limitations. The third essential element for all technology evaluation processes is the discovery of inherent technology limitations. Any inherent limitations need to be discovered during the initial technology feasibility study, as these limitations constrain the technology's ability to meet customer needs or otherwise impose additional technology or product design requirements.

For example, a resistive ribbon technology development team for a new typewriter learned that two adjacent resistive elements had to be "on" to ensure acceptable print quality. This technology limitation dictated a limit for the minimum print width of the typewriter [Voit, 1988].

In addition to the memory and microprocessor speed factors previously mentioned, *interoperability* is a potential limitation for software technologies. Customers often want to use a new product as part of an interdependent set of items. That is, the new product may be intended for use as part of an overall document preparation and distribution system that includes a word processor, a printer, a copier, a fax machine, and electronic mail. The inability to interface with relevant technology in the operational environment may not be an inherent limitation, but if the effort required to develop needed interoperability is beyond what can be justified, it may be considered an inherent limitation nonetheless. If so, the choice of technology for the new product must account for customers' concern for the new product's ability to work together with other products in the customers' environment.

Technology Selection

Customer Criteria Used in Selection. In the most successful projects, technology selection and evaluation criteria are strongly based on customer needs for performance, quality, reliability, and cost. Technology team members had a good understanding of customer needs for which the technology was being developed. (Customer requirements may not be very familiar to some technology developers.) A technology's cost was used only to the extent that proposed customers were perceived to consider cost as important; quality and reliability of the technology generally were emphasized more than cost. The teams used customer criteria not only for selection, but also used them during the Technology Feasibility Verification step to assess how well the developed technology met customer needs.

Early Technology Selection. In most cases involving a new technology, the technology selection process reveals the need for other related technological developments. Thus, each new technology not only needs to be evaluated to reveal these additional technology needs but also needs to be selected early enough in the development program to allow sufficient time for the additional technology development. For example, the successful development of a resistive ribbon typewriter required not only the development of resistive ribbon technology but advances in tungsten manufacturing technology so that the resistive ribbon printhead could be manufactured successfully [Voit, 1988]. The technology dependency noted above can be avoided *only* by making a conscious decision at the start of the program to use only established technologies in the new product.

The early selection of software technologies involves not only product technologies but development process technologies as well. The term "software engineering environment" refers to the set of automated support tools (also known as computer-aided software engineering [CASE] tools) used to support a development method in a given application domain. CASE tools may be freestanding, well integrated, or non-existent for various methods and applications, and the maturity of available software engineering environments may be a factor in product technology selection.

The Consideration of Several Candidates. The systematic evaluation of several technology candidates increases the probability of selecting the most appropriate technology and restricts the tendency to overpursue the first potential concept (thus avoiding the "Eureka" syndrome). Generally, both current and new technologies should be considered, as shown in figure 5.2. The hardware developed during this activity may be known as a "concept demonstrator" and is built primarily to assess the ability of potential technologies to meet basic requirements. (A successful concept demonstrator is not the end to the Technology Selection and Development phase; there is significantly more work to be done.)

New technologies are developed only enough to enable the team to make a good technology selection; the time required to develop the technology to an adequate state must be balanced with the need to select the technology early enough to complete its development. Subsequent efforts are then focused solely on development and verification of the selected technology.

New versus Existing Technology Considerations. The Technology Selection and Development phase can be affected dramatically by whether new or existing technology is selected. As shown in figure 5.2, selecting a new technology requires that it be developed so that the technology will function properly in a product or process environment. Issues related to this difference between new and existing technology selection must be considered. The fundamental issue to consider is that new technology development and verification takes much longer than does the verification of a current technology. Thus, fast-track projects that have accelerated product development schedules need to avoid selecting new technologies when suffcent time has not been scheduled for the needed technology development.

In one case study, a successful product had to be developed quickly to save a firm from bankruptcy liquidation. To minimize development time, a conscious decision was made at the project's start to use only established technologies in the new product. The selection of appropriate, established technologies enabled the development team to meet its accelerated schedule and deliver a highly profitable automated magnetic tape cartridge library [Abbott, 1988].

In addition to the fundamental decision to use new versus existing technology, a project team must decide whether to make, use, or buy the selected technology. For new technology, two options are available: make or buy. A firm may choose to make the technology itself, or it may buy the technology development from an outside supplier. Internal development is risky because of the unknowns; external development is even riskier due to the decreased visibility into the development process.

For existing technology, two options apply: use or buy. A company may use (or, more accurately, "reuse") an existing implementation (e.g., a subsystem or component) from a previous development effort. Alternatively, a company may buy off-the-shelf technology from an outside supplier.

Although all such decisions will not be made during the Technology Selection and Development phase, some of these decisions have a fundamental bearing on the viability of the product idea and the length of the development schedule.

Problems with Using Only Existing Technologies. Clark and Fujimoto's study [1991] of the automobile industry revealed that, on average, 38 percent of a new US automobile model's components are off-the-shelf parts, compared to only 18 percent such parts in new Japanese models. The hazard of using only existing technologies and components is that it is more difficult to provide the product with a competitive advantage. Some critics, for example, have charged that the overuse of existing parts led US firms to introduce new models that looked too much like their previous models and may have put them at a competitive disadvantage [*The Economist*, August 3, 1991, pp.64 – 5].

New Technology Risks. Technology problems must be considered as much more serious than product design problems. In complex products, new technologies may interact adversely with other new and existing technologies used elsewhere. Therefore, a new technology's compatibility with other technologies should be evaluated early. Failure to ensure that all selected technologies are compatible during the technology phase may result in an unwelcome and expensive surprise in the product design and evaluation phase.

New Technology Development

If a new technology is selected, it must be developed to a feasible state for design and manufacture before it can be used in a product. Three essential elements greatly enhance the quality of new technology development.

The Maximization of the Operating Space. The primary task in the New Technology Development step is to expand the operating space so that the technology is adequately robust. A range of values for the technology's critical variables are found that allow the widest possible variation in those values while still obtaining the desired level of output. The engineering targets and tolerances for the product design are derived from this range. Multivariate statistical testing procedures, such as design of experiments or Taguchi methods, can be very useful tools for this task. (Taguchi methods provide structured approaches for engineering experimentation. Peace [1993] provides a good explanation of the Taguchi approach.)

Variability Minimization. Effective control over the available operating space can be attained by minimizing the variability of the critical variables. For example, the hot roll fuser technology mentioned earlier was enhanced by developing a precise temperature measurement and control system accurate to 1° C.

Accurate temperature control helped to ensure reliable copy fusing even though the fuser functions properly only within a narrow temperature range [Wilson, 1979].

Simultaneous Product and Process Technology Development. New product technology development often necessitates the development of new process technologies to manufacture the new product hardware. And because requirements and limitations of one affect the other, product and process technology development must be closely interrelated.

The success of a manufacturing system design is predicated largely on its ability to control critical manufacturing processes. Development of this control capability is initiated during the Technology Selection and Development phase. Indeed, difficulties in controlling new processes can cause long delays in the development of a product containing new technologies. Thus, new process technologies should be developed simultaneously and in conjunction with new product technologies. For example, an inkjet printer project required the development of not only an inkjet printhead, but also a new sealing technology to eliminate printhead air gaps [Boeller, 1988].

While the emphasis of this chapter is directed toward product technology development, the same essential elements apply equally to process technology development. Successful new technology manufacturing processes are characterized, controlled, and "capable" (this term is specifically defined in the Manufacturing System Design phase chapter). Key process technology attributes must be quantified and well understood; they are not a black art. Limitations of selected manufacturing processes must be known.

Technology Feasibility Verification

After selection and development, the final task is to verify that the technology indeed is ready for the Product or Process Design phase and to ensure that all requirements are achieved. Exiting the Technology Selection and Development phase before completing this verification step can be a large technical risk; the composite wing example mentioned earlier shows that failing to verify a technology before design can be very expensive in both development time and cost.

Critical Variables Defined, Quantified, and Targeted. All operating factors related to the technology must be known and quantified. Target values for critical variables must be selected. Operating spaces for these variables must be defined. All necessary design and performance data must be available to accomplish a complete product and process design.

Critical Requirements Demonstrated. All technology requirements related to performance, quality, life, and reliability are demonstrated successfully with prototype hardware. Materials and manufacturing processes critical to successful technology use are identified and, if necessary, developed. The prototype hardware has all the relevant controls, instrumentation, and features that are necessary for proper technology operation. Development results compare favorably to the goals that were established to begin the project.

The Technology Feasibility Statement. The Technology Feasibility Statement is a formal assessment of the capabilities, requirements, and limitations for the selected technology. It summarizes the technology effort. The statement includes a recommendation as to whether to proceed with product design. If the recommendation is "go," the statement provides the necessary technical data to use the technology in a product design – especially information related to the critical variables just discussed.

For example, the hot roll fuser technology team constructed a technology feasibility statement to conclude its technology effort. Along with a recommendation to proceed with a copier design, the statement included design and performance information, special material selections and manufacturing methods, and a life estimate. A working configuration with the necessary instrumentation and controls was shown to have a sufficiently large operating space for acceptable quality. In short, the technology was verified for use and necessary design requirements were provided [Wilson, 1979].

Summary

The Technology Selection and Development phase is critical to the timely development of superior quality products. The essential elements for this phase are described in this chapter to enable the *correct selection, proper development, and adequate verification* of product and process technologies.

The most effective technology developers strive to create robust products and processes. They carry technology experiments beyond a fragile "gee whiz" stage to characterize and control the technology. They discover critical parameters, establish an operating space, and find any technology limitations.

The technology selection can dramatically affect the product development process. If a new technology is selected, personnel, resources, and time must be allocated for new technology development. In all cases, deliberate engineering action and leadership are imperative to demonstrate the feasibility of a technology. The most important work product resulting from the Technology Selection and Development phase is the Technology Feasibility Statement.

References

Abbott, Tom (1988), "Improving the Product Development Process," notes from ASME short course, "Case Studies of Engineering and Manufacturing Methods for Superior Results," Atlanta, GA, April 18 – 19, 1988.

Boeller, C. A., et al. (1988), "High-Volume Microassembly of Color Thermal Inkjet Printheads and Cartridges," *Hewlett-Packard Journal*, August 1988, pp. 32 – 40.

Carley, W. M. (1989), "Wing Flap: Contractor's Mishaps in New Technology Made the Navy Seethe," *The Wall Street Journal*, January 11, 1989, pp. A1, A6.

Clark, Kim B., and Takahiro Fujimoto (1991), *Product Development Performance: Strategy, Organization, and Management in the World Auto Industry*, Harvard Business School Press, Boston.

Peace, Glen Stuart (1993), *Taguchi Methods: A Hands-On Approach*, Addison-Wesley, Reading, MA.

Voit, W. (1988), "Resistive Ribbon Technology," notes from case study presented at the University of Tennessee, Knoxville, TN, April 14, 1988.

Wilson, Clement C. (1979), "A New Fuser Technology for Electro-photographic Printing Machines," *Journal of Applied Photographic Engineering*, Summer 1979, pp. 148 – 156.

"Rusting Away: America's Car Industry," *The Economist*, London, England, August 3, 1991, pp. 64 – 65.

Selected Bibliography

Wilson, Clement C., and Michael E. Kennedy (1990), "Some Essential Elements for Product Technology Selection and Development," *Proceedings of the Second International Conference on Management of Technology*, University of Miami, Miami, FL, February 1990.

Wilson, Clement C., and Michael E. Kennedy (1991), "Improving the Product Development Process," Chapter 18 in *Competing Globally Through Customer Value: The Management of Strategic Suprasystems*, M. J. Stahl and G. M. Bounds (eds.), New York: Quorum Books, 1991.

CHAPTER 6

FINAL PRODUCT DEFINITION
AND PROJECT TARGETS

The development team enters the Final Product Definition and Project Targets phase with a great deal of information about what customers value and what technical capabilities exist to meet customer needs. By removing itself from this phase, the firm's upper management has provided significant commitments (and resources) to the project team, if the product is approved to move forward in the development process. Within this phase is the first of two major "go, no-go" decision points. (Another such decision point resides at the end of the Product Design and Evaluation phase.)

Upon entering this phase, the product's target customers have been identified and their future needs projected and ranked in order of importance. Competing products and processes have been benchmarked to gain an understanding of what the product must be and do to be superior to competitive offerings, present and future. Potential product and process technologies have been investigated and tested to determine what performance levels they can reliably attain. Technology Feasibility Statements have been written to define the capabilities of these technologies with respect to their use in the new product.

All of this information is combined and integrated during this phase to define the new product. As the product itself is defined, resources and development time are allocated to support the product's development. The product's market and business potential are estimated formally to assess the product's value toward meeting the firm's long-term objectives. By iterating the process and by making the appropriate tradeoffs among the product definition, targets for major cost drivers, development time, and other factors, an acceptable business case is synthesized.

Milestone Goals

The first milestone goal for the Final Product Definition and Project Targets phase is *to define a final (or "frozen") base product plus optional derivative products.* The base product definition remains frozen throughout the remainder of the development process; planned derivatives enable enhancements while allowing the product definition to remain frozen.

The second goal is *to set targets for the project's engineering, manufacturing, marketing, and scheduling to produce a successful "business case" for the product.* The targeting process enables a financially viable business plan to be synthesized through the setting of challenging (yet attainable) limits for the product's engineering, manufacturing, marketing, and service expenses.

The third goal is *to gain higher management commitment and support for the two milestone results attained above* – that is, to pass the Product Concept Review.

Process Description

The Final Product Definition and Project Targets phase commences with the conclusion of the Customer Future Needs Projection and the Technology Selection and Development phases (both product and process), as is shown in figure 6.1.

The basic items needed to complete the Final Product Definition and Project Targets phase are shown in figure 6.2. Well-defined customer needs and demonstrated technologies from previous phases are brought forward concurrently to be integrated into a coherent product definition. The product definition is accompanied by a related set of project targets, which synthesize the marketing, schedule (milestones), and all project cost objectives into an acceptable business plan.

Essential Elements

The essential elements for the Final Product Definition and Project Targets phase encourage the team to define the product

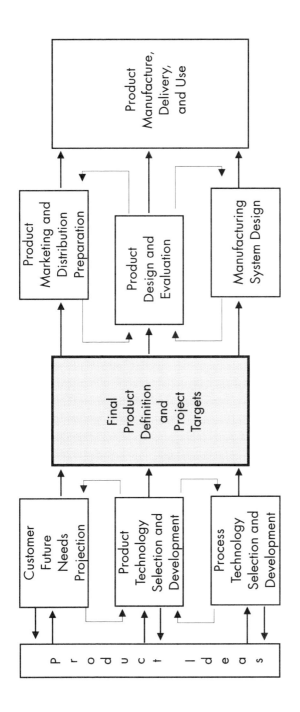

Figure 6.1. The Final Product Definition and Project Targets phase within the overall product development process.

97

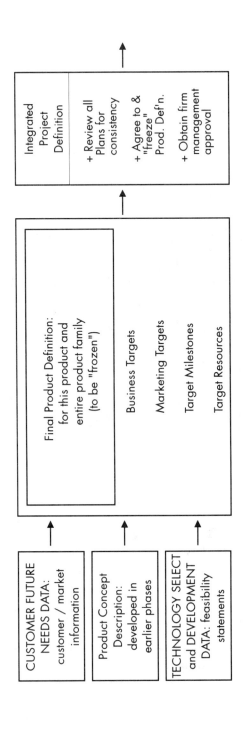

Figure 6.2. The Final Product Definition and Project Targets phase.

and supporting targets in a way that is the most likely to aid the product's success. These elements are:

- The synthesization of an acceptable business plan by iterating the project targets for the engineering, manufacturing, and marketing and distribution plans;
- Stable, complete targets for product and process are established;
- The definition of critical design constraints; and
- The freezing of the product definition for the project duration at the end of the phase.

The Synthesis of an Acceptable Business Plan by Iterating Project Targets

The first essential element is to synthesize an acceptable business plan by iterating the project targets for the engineering, manufacturing, and marketing and distribution aspects of the project. The *synthesis* of the business case is very important: *It is a major change from what often happens in functional organizations, which analyze the cost inputs and then either accept or reject the product.* The integrated development team is in the best position to make the changes and tradeoffs needed to synthesize a successful product development program. Japanese firms have used this technique for years to deliver cost-competitive products in cut-throat consumer markets. It has also been used extensively by US firms that are competing effectively in the world marketplace.

The Establishment of Stable, Complete Targets for Product and Processes

Comprehensive requirements and goals are developed for both the product itself and for the processes used in its manufacture. A superior product definition describes the core benefits that must be provided to create the complete product. In addition to critical features and product performance parameters, it includes relevant product and process quality goals, target product cost, and significant human interface design needs. Effective use of information gathered in the Technology Selection and Development and Customer Future Needs Projection phases is imperative for creating a successful product definition.

The product definition, which may be referred to as a "product requirements list" in some firms, provides the fundamental basis for the product design. In the successful case studies, stable, comprehensive requirements and goals were developed for both the product *and* its manufacturing processes. The product definition is established and frozen before detailed product and process design activities begin.

The Definition of Critical Design Objectives and Constraints

Superior product definitions also include any special requirements, such as design for assembly goals, the ability of the design to be used as a basis for a family of products, essential design standards requirements (such as the need for UL approval), manufacturing restrictions, and so forth. In many of the cases, these design targets were prioritized based on the importance of each particular objective.

Design for assembly goals, such as "no screws allowed," were established in the product definition for the IBM Proprinter, a popular, low-cost dot-matrix printer. With this objective implanted as an integral part of the product's definition, the Proprinter established a benchmark for design for assembly that has rarely been exceeded. For an HP inkjet printer, one product requirement was that the printhead needed to be designed as a disposable module – the economical manufacture of this key module was a key technical process for the product.

The Freezing of the Product Definition for the Project Duration at the End of the Phase

Product definitions of successful products are frozen to eliminate the continuous redesign that inevitably results when the product definition is repeatedly changed during the Product Design phase. This freezing also works to constrain urges by the team to solve design problems by changing the product definition.

Thus, a product definition should be frozen once it is approved. Studies made within IBM repeatedly showed that unstable product requirements were a major cause of product development delays. However, the act of freezing the product definition dramatically increases the importance of establishing the proper definition *the first time* and of completing the project per its defined milestones. A product definition that plans for a series of derivative products, each with incremental improvements or new features, can be used to stimulate the market throughout the product's market life while still allowing the base product definition to remain frozen.

The Final Product Definition

The product definition provides the basis for the product's design and serves as the primary objectives statement for the product. It is referred to as "final" because this definition is not to be changed once it is approved at the end of this phase. The product definition is built from the product concept definition, which was established originally during the Product Ideas phase and was perhaps modified during the Customer Future Needs Projection phase. The product definition addresses four critical product areas:

- The focus of the product (its key objectives);
- The basic product concept, including critical features and performance;
- The product family (the core product plus any desired derivatives); and
- A characterization or ranking of the definition items (relative priorities of the definition's components and how they relate to each other).

The Focus of the Product

To find the product's focus, answer this question: What are the key objectives for this product?

The Basic Product Concept: Critical Features and Performance

Features. To establish the basic product concept, one defines

101

the critical features and performance from the customer's perspective. All product features should be included in the product definition. In addition to primary product features, administrative or maintenance features should be identified. Products with embedded software, for example, may require security, audit, diagnostic, or recovery features.

Required interfaces to other systems are identified. If the software component receives information from an external data source, the form and integrity of the external data must be defined. If the integrity of externally supplied data cannot be ensured, data validation and error-handling features must be included in the product definition.

Performance.   Critical performance items, from a user's point of view, are to be defined, particularly for the human interface. This is important because design requirements, such as microprocessor and memory needs, will depend on how performance requirements are defined. Dimensions of performance that generally must be specified include response time, throughput, capacity, task complexity, and system load.

Quantified Quality Measures.   Quantitative values for critical product characteristics, based on the measures developed earlier, are set as targets for the product (and process) design.

Product Quality Objectives.   Product reliability requirements in appropriate units of measure should be established. For the hardware, mean time to failure or its reciprocal failure/time are meaningful measurements of reliability. Another meaningful measurement is "uptime," the time that the machine is available for use. For software, the reliability also might be expressed as mean time to failure, where time is measured in customer uses. A "use," then, must be defined in meaningful terms for the product.

Modularity Needs.   Modularity requirements enable hardware and software to be reused in derivative products. In particular, software should generally be designed for *reusability* in derivative products, *portability* to other processor platforms in product upgrades, and *maintainability* for ease of modification. Generally, hardware subsystems should also be modular, unless space or weight requirements prevent their use.

Product Family

The Use of Derivatives and Options.   The concept of a product family (i.e., the development of a base product followed at later dates by a series of derivative products) allows a major product development pitfall to be avoided. In virtually every project, good ideas about product features and functions arise after the product design is well under way. To add these ideas to the base product would delay the product's introduction to market. However, if derivative products have been planned, these new ideas can be applied to the most appropriate derivative product without delaying the introduction of the base product.

Using the product family strategy enables the team to add product options over time and to define when it will reach customers. Introduction of these new derivative products and options can be timed to coincide with the marketing need to present customers with new options. Customers often will not take time to see a salesperson unless he or she "has something new since the last time you were here." Planned, derivative changes to the product, made on a periodic basis, can substantially improve the ability to market that product. (Consider, for example, the annual changes made to automobile models.)

The Grouping of Derivatives and Options.   To reduce the number of customer option combinations (while still enabling customers to have selections), the Boeing Company has adopted a "catalog" approach to some airframe options. Customers choose customization options from an available catalog of options, instead of specifying each option individually. By taking this approach, Boeing was able reduce the number of special-order options from about 600 to 50, with a corresponding reduction in manufacturing complexity.

Option standardization and grouping also have reduced the number of available options in automobiles. Many customers actually appreciate not having to haggle with an obnoxious salesperson over each individual option during the purchase process. Since the manufacturing facility can generally add the options less expensively at the factory than can the dealer, a full options package can be delivered to the customer at a lower price.

Characterize and Rank Definition Items

The customer priorities developed during the Future Customer Needs phase are used to set the rankings within the product definition. Lower ranking goals and preferences can be carried forward as well so that some of them can be incorporated as development proceeds. The operational usage profile developed during the assessment of customer needs can also be used in the ranking of elements in the product definition.

The importance of a meaningful final product definition is underscored by the comments about arbitrary specifications made by Ron Randall, quality manager at Texas Instruments: "We experience costly delays relative to our attempts at meeting arbitrary specs, and specs that are not even relevant to the needs." Most experienced product developers have encountered this problem.

Business Targets

Synthesis versus Analysis of the Business Plan

The synthesis of business targets for creating the needed financial returns from a product development project is a very powerful concept. *Project teams that have used this concept have made major product design and manufacturing improvements to meet aggressive product targets and have realized cost reductions far greater than anything previously thought possible.* An integrated product team that is given the ability to take whatever engineering, manufacturing, marketing directions are needed to produce and deliver an affordable, high value product can use this technique to great advantage.

For example, firms with large marketing organizations

learned that development teams could develop and use alternate marketing channels that were dramatically less costly than the firm's standard product marketing methods. Throughout the 1980s various IBM divisions evaded the company's own marketing, manufacturing, and real estate organizations because they were unaffordable. (The IBM personal computer was the first product to successfully break out from IBM's unaffordable business practices.) As this book is being written, IBM is still making major organizational cuts to bring its costs in line and is studying intensely the improved product development methods of firms such as Lexmark International, which has been very successful since being sold by IBM in the early 1990s.

Many large, unaffordable organizations have attempted to finance their corporate overhead problems by forcing products to meet unrealistic, noncompetitive financial return criteria or to pay excessive overhead allocations. These excessively high costs lead a firm either to cancel most of its development projects (because most or all of these products cannot meet financial criteria) or to "cost reduce" a product's features to the point that products are not competitive. Canceling products reduces future cash flow and earnings, which eventually pushes the firm into major financial problems. The synthesis approach can keep good new product efforts from being killed by the firm's own excessive overhead costs, while also forcing the unaffordable parent organization to confront those costs directly.

While profitability (or business) analysis is fundamental to each product development project, it should not be used as the only basis for decision making. A given product development project may enable the firm to win new customers, to gain substantial market share (and thus to perhaps make an expensive marketing effort affordable), to keep its present customers during a transition period, or enable the firm to earn the leadership of its industry. Projects also provide a needed environment for "product development learning" (e.g., discovering new customer needs and controlling new manufacturing processes) and for practicing critical skills (such as designing or testing new products). Learning experiences, in particular, are critically important to the firm's long-term success, because without the requisite learning, the firm will eventually find itself incapable – technically, managerially, and otherwise – of developing *any* products.

The Effect of Associated Revenues and Costs

Other income and costs can significantly affect the business picture associated with the new product. For example, US computer manufacturers earn a quarter of their revenues from the service and maintenance of the products they sell. Profit margins on service contracts can be as high as 50 percent [*The Economist*, June 20, 1992, p.69]. On the other hand, another product can require extensive (i.e., expensive) product support services to make the product successful.

The risk in including service and maintenance revenues as profit sources, of course, is that it potentially rewards design, manufacturing, and service errors. As Bloch and Conrad have stated, "Making a profit on product design errors or on the lack of product reliability does not provide a strong incentive to improve customer satisfaction" [Bloch and Conrad, 1988, p.7]. In some industries, Japanese firms have reminded US manufacturers of this lesson the hard way. The television maker Zenith once advertised its sets as "easy to service," only to watch purchasers pay a premium for much more reliable Sony sets that eliminated most servicing needs. Similarly, Japanese automobile owners found that not having to return their vehicles for repair was much more satisfying than was obtaining free warranty work from US automobile makers. The lesson here is that the product's reliability and quality objectives must be made equal or better than the best available, even though there is indeed money to be made in service. Products that are as service-free as possible are the most pleasing to customers.

Another source of revenue is replaceable supplies in products. The classic, historical case of this in consumer products is the nonelectric razor, where razor blade sales earn the profits and the sale of the associated handle and case often do not. This concept sometimes extends into innovative products such as printers, where users periodically must fill or replace containers of the toner consumed in printing. In many of today's copiers and laser printers, users are also replacing an entire electrophotographic module when they replace their toner cartridge. This module comprises approximately one-third of the machine and contains the components that get the most contaminated and that have the shortest life. By having the customer replace this module periodically with the toner refill, the printer becomes virtually service free. The profitability of these supplies can be very significant. It must be included in the product's business case *and not as a separate business case*.

Core Components and Economies of Scale

While each product family (or "line") is usually considered separately from the others, one important cross-family consideration is how the firm's manufacturing processes and volume can be used to create an economic advantage across those product lines. For example, copier firms are well poised for expanding into laser printers. Canon has a laser printer product family (including the engine for the Hewlett-Packard laser printers) that uses many of the same supplies, electrophotographic modules, fusers, and paper-handling equipment as does its personal copier product line. In Canon's case, laser printer manufacturing becomes merely an extension of its copier efforts, since both are based upon a common electrophotographic technology and have been designed to use common parts. This cross-family manufacturing base provides strong advantages over other firms (such as Lexmark International or even Hewlett-Packard) who do not have an existing copier manufacturing base.

The issue is that the consideration of key core technologies and core manufacturing bases is important to the business success of an enterprise. Under certain conditions, a firm may have to introduce a product with minimal profit potential in order to build the strategic technology and manufacturing base needed to launch a variety of related products. Profit margins grow over time as the additional product families are subsequently launched.

Clearly, product development projects are multifaceted, so to judge them solely on a single facet (such as their financial return) is unwise. Hayes, Wheelwright, and Clark [1988, p.76] have provided this great perspective on financial evaluation: "The most profitable time for a company often occurs between the time it stops investing and when it goes out of business." Firms who pursue superior product development are planning on being in business for the long term.

Marketing Targets

The marketing targets provide the basis for marketing and distribution preparation activities that start once this phase is completed. (See chapter 7 for a more detailed discussion of these activities.) The "4 Ps" of marketing – product, price, place, and promotion – are tied to these target values. The key targets relate directly to the business plan. For example, the target price and the estimated quantity demand for the product form the basis for the business plan's sales income target. At the same time, expense levels for distribution channel development and promotion (advertising) are set as target values, which serve to limit the marketing expenses for the product.

These targets are extremely important for triggering the most appropriate marketing preparations for the product. Many US firms found that not only were their manufacturing costs too high, but their marketing costs were as well. The task for the team's marketing-oriented members is to find the new marketing and distribution methods that are consistent with (i.e., affordable within) these targets if the firm's marketing-as-usual practices prove too costly. Sales and distribution methods for business machines have changed dramatically over the last 20 years for just this reason. Personal computers are now sold through a wide array of channels – via catalogs, general retailers, authorized computer dealers, 1-800 numbers, and even television shopping networks.

Products that are very service intensive may require a study and targeting of product life cycle costs. Copier customers, for example, must take service (or service/maintenance contract) costs into account when deciding whether to purchase a new machine. Therefore, target costs for maintenance and service are important in this product line.

Harmon and Peterson [1990] claim that many Japanese firms assume that they will attain dominant market shares when planning new products and processes. Such aggressive goals tend to be self-fulfilling, as the goals drive the team to lowest cost, highest quality processes. Risk can be minimized by following a modular manufacturing strategy, where incrementally sized manufacturing modules can be gradually added to meet increased demand.

Project Milestone Targets

Avoiding the Pitfall of the "Unobtainable Schedule"

Target milestones (including the target date for product introduction) are as important as any project target. One of the greatest pitfalls in product development is management's demand for, and the team's acceptance of, an unobtainably fast schedule [Wilson, 1991]. Because many US firms are trying to catch up to foreign competition, there is great pressure to shorten the new product development process. Many CEOs are demanding immediate development cycle reductions to match the latest Japanese record, as quoted by the firm's consultant. They do not appear to understand the difference between establishing a schedule for an innovative product that incorporates new technology and setting the much shorter schedule for a derivative product containing no new technology. Although schedules of 18 months are being quoted as the norm for the Japanese-developed derivative products, Toyota's Lexus automobile was under development for six years. Figure 6.3 illustrates the large range of product development time that can be realized, depending upon the type of product to be developed. It is interesting to note that development time is also the length of time needed for a competitor to catch up.

Firms that force teams to commit to unattainable schedules often find not only that the schedule date has been missed by a huge margin, but also that the rushed product is not ready for

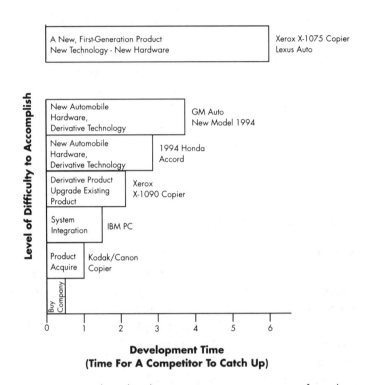

Figure 6.3. Product development times versus types of product.

production and customer use. The penalty for promising to meet an unobtainable schedule and missing it can be much worse than what occurs by promising and meeting a somewhat longer schedule. Typical problems that cause teams to miss schedules include continual changes to parts tooling (caused by having to start tooling too early with an immature product design) and a low yield from a new (and inadequately developed) process technology. If much hard tooling has to be changed, a year can easily be lost on a schedule. However, setting an attainable schedule of 29 months, instead of an unobtainable 24 months, can make an enormous difference in the team's ability to avoid the repeated rework to tools and processes, if the extra time is used properly – to complete technology development and to finish the product design.

By the same token, firms that work to a 4-year schedule while their competition works successfully to a 3-year schedule will inevitably find themselves missing market windows because their products are always late. Walking the line between the two extremes takes great judgment and skill on the part of the product development team.

How does one know what is obtainable and what is not? Hewlett-Packard keeps records of its projects and compares proposed new project schedules to the best previous development times for similar products. Only if new development methods can be identified that will shorten the schedule is a shorter schedule approved for the new product. Thus, when they shorten a schedule, they know what will be done to shorten it. At the same time, HP development teams are challenged to schedule against the fastest "break-even times" that they can meet successfully.

In general, management of a project team can avoid the unobtainable schedule pitfall by:

- Knowing the complexity of each product under development and its relative percentage of new and derivative technology;
- Examining past performance in meeting the schedule for products of different levels of complexity;
- Keeping records on each product regarding its complexity and schedule (the HP method); and
- Making changes on the basis of past schedules and managing those changes in order to meet the new schedule.

Milestones to Use

The obvious milestones start with six months after product launch (when the production process is passed from the development team to the firm's manufacturing organization) and work backwards through the product development phases described in this book.

Within the Product Design and Evaluation phase (which is often the longest in the development of an innovative product), an iterative process will be used to ensure controlled refinement of the product. The functions that are to be implemented in each iteration should be identified, and target dates for each of those iterations should be established as milestones. This early planning and coordination of hardware and software design processes allow priorities and risks to be understood and managed from the beginning.

Project Reviews

The number of reviews needed in the project milestones depends a great deal upon the needs of the team. Too many reviews waste time and put the team on the defensive, while too few reviews may allow critical problems to linger too long without resolution. Team leaders must assess these conflicting issues when defining the quantity and timing of their reviews.

Critical milestones occur at the ends of the Product and Process Technology Selection and Development phases. The formal presentation of technical feasibility statements is important. If this review is not done, a technology may be presumed to be developed to an adequate state, only to be found fragile after it is implemented in production. One example of this problem occurred in the late 1980s when low production yields for a Motorola microcontroller caused the launch of a new Hewlett-Packard personal computer to be delayed for over a year.

Other major project reviews occur at ends of the Final Product Definition and Project Targets and Product Design and Evaluation phases. The software reviews that occur in conjunction with each iterative cycle of the Product Design and Evaluation phase include: a top-level specification review, a verification review of design against specifications, and a test plan review. (These reviews are discussed in chapter 7.)

Target Resources

The importance of using an effective, integrated team has been emphasized over and over throughout this book. There is no more important essential element than an integrated product development team led by an effective team leader with authority. The technical adequacy of the team is best achieved by staffing the team with the smallest number of the most experienced and broadest technical people that are available. This requirement is important to keep bureaucracy and learning curves to a minimum. It is much more effective to put together a lean staff of experienced personnel and to have them work 50 – 60+ hours per week than to attempt to work 40 hours per week with a much larger, inexperienced team. Product development experience cannot be substituted through larger numbers of inexperienced people. The larger, less-experienced team will fall behind the experienced team and will eventually have to work longer hours in an attempt to catch up. Of course, it is important that team members be able to work together compatibly. This requirement is much easier said than done, but it is a condition of participating on the team.

The software team should have a leader who works with hardware counterparts compatibly to ensure that hardware-software codesign yields the best product tradeoff decisions. Additional leadership on the software team is provided by a chief designer and a chief certification testing engineer. Each of those leaders has a small team for development and testing work. If the system is too large for a small team, subsystems in the top-level architecture should be developed by separate, small teams.

The Definition and Targets Review

The goal of the Product Definition and Targets Review step is to ensure that the product definition and targets are complete, so that a competitive, quality product design can be completed on time. This review is shown in figure 6.4. This is a major review and is extremely important, because the base product may not be changed after it is approved – it is frozen at the end of this review.

Like many development activities, this review may be an iterative process. Thus, the team may develop and review product definition and targets several times before presenting the

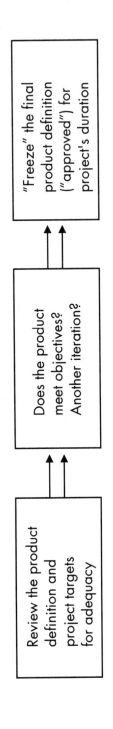

Figure 6.4. The Product Definition and Project Targets Review process.

final objectives for approval. The first general task is to review the adequacy of the product definition and project targets by determining the answers to these questions: Do the product and the targets meet all objectives? Should it proceed or is another iteration required?

Meeting *all* the objectives means just that. This particularly applies to the synthesis of business objectives. In a competitive environment, each area may think that it is being pressured to do too much with too little to meet the overall business objectives. This situation can become very tense if each area requires substantial innovation to meet their targets and they are not sure that they can do it. Team leadership is critical during this time to build the consensus that allows each area to stretch rather equally without generating too big of a failure risk. Iterating the objectives until a balanced set of targets can be reached is required.

Once the objectives are approved, the team and the firm's management freeze the final product definition for the project's duration. This is the major decision point for the team. After the team agrees, they carry the product definition and targets to top management for approval to move the project forward. Approval to proceed commits the team and management explicitly to completing the effort through to the Product Manufacture phase, unless otherwise defined in the milestone targets.

Summary

In summary, the output documents of this phase are the final product definition and the synthesized business case with the project targets that support it. Within the targets are the project time milestones that describe the implementation schedule for the project from staffing to launch date plus six months – in short, the function, costs, development schedule, and business case of the proposed product. This information is taken to the highest level of management to get commitment to staff the project for successful implementation.

References

Bloch, Erich, and Kathy Prager Conrad (1988), "Manufacturing Systems: An Overview," *Design and Analysis of Integrated Manufacturing Systems*, W. Dale Compton, ed., National Academy of Engineering, Washington, DC.

Harmon, Roy L., and Leroy D. Peterson (1990), *Reinventing the Factory: Productivity Breakthroughs in Manufacturing Today*, The Free Press, New York.

Hayes, Robert H., Wheelwright, Steven C., and Clark, Kim B. (1988), *Dynamic Manufacturing*, The Free Press, New York.

Wilson, Clement C. (1991), "Potential Pitfalls of Concurrent Engineering: How to Avoid the Risks," *Concurrent Engineering*, January/February 1991.

"Lotus-eater," *The Economist*, London, England, June 20, 1992, pp. 66 – 67.

CHAPTER 7

PRODUCT DESIGN AND EVALUATION

The Product Design and Evaluation phase, highlighted in figure 7.1, is where the major engineering and testing of the product are performed. It starts with the creation of the Product Design Specification and ends with complete drawings, specifications, and critical parameter information for manufacture. These work products are the results of carefully controlled design iterations and designed tests that evaluate product performance over its range of use and environment and beyond. *This phase of the product development process is critical to the success of the product, because it is here that robust products with high customer value are created.* This phase requires a creative and detailed effort to design, build, and test prototypes that are representative of the final manufactured product. Inadequate design and/or testing can result in unpleasant surprises when the final product is put into the customer's hands in the customer environment. Unexpected (but avoidable) product failures that arise either in manufacturing or in the hands of the customer are extremely expensive and have even put firms out of business.

The ability of Japanese firms to execute this portion of the product development process is generally superior to that of most US firms. The ability of Japanese industry to integrate product design with the manufacturing process design to create virtually error-free product performance and manufacturing replication is unmatched in the industrial world. Many of the "secrets" used by the competitive US firms who have demonstrated the ability to compete effectively with Japanese firms are provided throughout this chapter.

The material in this chapter is developed specifically for engineers; however, it is critically important that students and

118

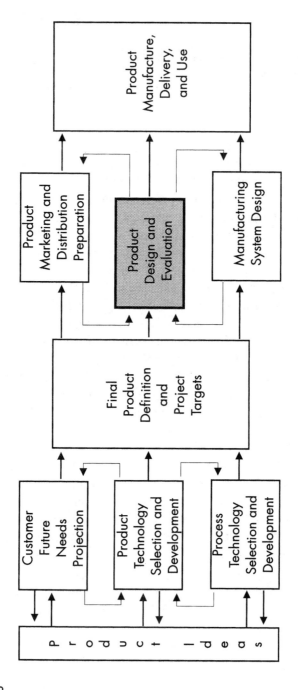

Figure 7.1. The Product Design and Evaluation phase within the overall product development process.

professionals from other backgrounds appreciate the amount and type of work that are required to develop an innovative product properly. The amount of work required varies enormously depending upon the type of product being developed – for example, whether it is a breakthrough product requiring large changes from previous products and large changes in the manufacturing processes or a derivative product requiring minor product and process changes. A major management task for the successful product development team is to understand the scope of the work to be done, plan and staff the project accordingly, and execute the plan systematically.

Today's superior products must have high customer value, be robust, and be brought to market in a timely manner. Many product development engineers would say that a rapid development cycle is contradictory to the development of a robust product with high customer value simply because more engineering work is usually required to bring forward new features and to guarantee robust performance. However, it *is* possible to have product value, product robustness, and process speed simultaneously – but the product development process must change from "business as usual" (i.e., sequential handoffs from one function to another) to make this possible.

All three attributes must be integrated and balanced to develop the successful product. For example, software and hardware engineering deadlines are on the critical path in bringing new products to market, and it is common for these efforts to be the cause of schedule and budget overruns. Software and hardware engineering need not be the most uncontrollable aspects of product development, however. Engineering development and testing can be approached as engineering practices that can be defined, controlled, and improved – as are other aspects of engineering.

A process that speeds up the product design and evaluation phase while at the same time delivering product customer value and product robustness is shown in this chapter.

Milestone Goals

The goals for the Product Design and Evaluation phase are simple, even though the phase itself is complex. These goals are to:

- Develop a complete Product Design Specification (PDS), translating the Final Product Definition into technical Specifications;
- Design, build, and test the product and subsystems by a controlled iteration process, thus developing a robust product by removing and preventing failure modes;
- Execute a comprehensive evaluation program, thereby verifying the designed product's value and fitness for manufacture and customer use;
- Plan and manage the Product Design and Evaluation phase activities so that the firm's product development is faster than that of competing products while still delivering a robust, high value product;
- Confirm the target estimates of the product's life cycle costs that support the successful business plan while solving any exceptional cost problems through appropriate actions; and
- Gain higher management support and financial commitment for product release to manufacturing by passing the Product Release Review.

Process Description

Figure 7.2 shows that the Product Design and Evaluation phase consists of five major activities, starting with the creation of the PDS and ending with product release to manufacturing. The second and third activities are concerned with design and the last two with evaluation. Thus, one can think of the overall phase as consisting of three major parts: specification, design, and evaluation.

The PDS, created in the first step of this phase, provides the technical description of all the customer requirements for the product. There may be no more important step in the entire

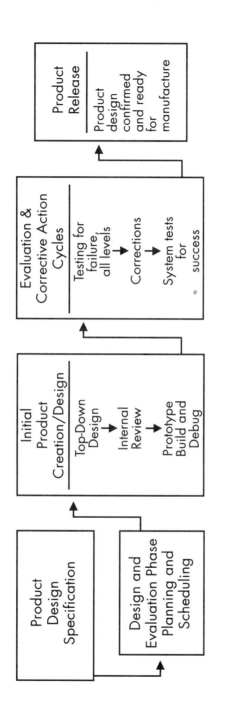

Figure 7.2. The Product Design and Evaluation phase.

product development process than the creation of a complete PDS. Many engineers resist this critical discipline of creating a written set of requirements for the product because they are so anxious to start the actual hardware and software design. The writing of the specification also appears bureaucratic to some. However, those who begin the design of a complex system before the PDS is complete invariably find that what they have designed is not what others expected them to have designed.

Design and evaluation efforts follow the completion of the PDS. Many firms organize their product design and evaluation activities in series; that is, they complete the design in its entirety before beginning any evaluation. Government contracts, in particular, are notorious for specifying that design and evaluation be performed sequentially. Development teams assume significant risks, however, by not performing any significant evaluation until after the design is completely finished. If major product failures occur during the evaluation that require substantial design changes to solve, the time and effort needed to fix the "finished" design will dramatically delay the introduction of the product to market. Firms that have competitive product development processes plan several cycles, or iterations, of design and evaluation.

The management and technical control of the development project are based on these iterations. The full design and evaluation program for the product is performed using a planned series of cumulative iterations. The minimal product is built during initial product creation. Additional user function is added in the next iteration and so on until all user functions have been implemented.

An iterative development process offers several advantages.

- Project risk can be managed through choices about which function gets the earliest attention. The most novel, complex, highly used, or poorly specified functions may be planned for early iterations. Other considerations in iteration planning may be early decisions on user interface, functional dependencies, and reliability allocation.

- Control of the development process is possible by comparing the performance in each iteration with quality standards.
- Customer feedback about the evolving product can be a planned part of the development program.

Essential Elements

The Product Design and Evaluation phase is the heart of the engineering activity that is required to ensure successful product function. Throughout our case studies of superior products, we find that engineers who create robust products during the Product Design phase place more emphasis on ensuring reliable product and process function than they do on achieving the minimum parts cost. Product cost is minimized by simplifying the design and matching the design to the appropriate manufacturing process, thereby reducing manufacturing and service times. The goal of the engineering effort is to create a product superior to the competition and one that meets the customers' value expectations.

The essential elements of this critical phase of the product development process:

- A comprehensive and concise PDS;
- Skilled design, manufacturing, and test engineers;
- A design margin;
- Design reviews;
- A comprehensive test program (including parts, subsystem, and system testing; a deliberate "tests-to-failure" evaluation; and stress testing);
- Effective test strategies; and
- Labeled and well-known critical parameters.

A Comprehensive and Concise Product Design Specification

The PDS is the complete description of the requirements of the product and the environment in which it is required to function. A comprehensive yet concise PDS provides everyone on the development team with a common reference about the full spectrum of product requirements. (The PDS is discussed further later in this chapter.)

Skilled and Experienced Design, Manufacturing, and Test Engineers

To achieve a superior product design, the development team must include experienced design and manufacturing engineers who have extensive knowledge of current parts manufacturing and assembly practices. In the case studies that used a design-for-manufacturing approach [Hadden, 1986; Baker et al., 1988; Abbott, 1988; Galatha, 1988], the design engineers worked closely with parts suppliers to ensure that part designs were compatible with intended manufacturing processes. Design engineers also received additional training in manufacturing techniques. In summary, both design and manufacturing knowledge must be within the project or be acquired.

Some major US firms are doing much of their product engineering work with temporary contract engineers in order to limit their manpower and reduce their benefit costs. This practice involves considerable risks, since the experience and training of their engineers is being delegated to the contracting company. For example, one office equipment company that hired temporary contract engineers based upon their ability to use a complex solid-modeling computer-aided-design program found that they had hired aerospace engineers to design office machinery. These engineers had come from an aerospace environment that had been completely specialized by function, and the process of working with the manufacturer of the parts was foreign to them. They were used to drawing up the parts, "tossing them over the wall to manufacturing," and counting on that group to work out the problems. The result was a design that was very expensive to manufacture and that eventually had to be scrapped. Other engineers with office equipment design and manufacturing skills had to be borrowed from other projects to rescue the project.

Experience is equally important for the test engineers. A few experienced testing engineers are required on the team to ensure that the testing is done efficiently and effectively to find and solve critical problems. The testing engineers can be the primary planners and trainers of the other engineers and technicians who conduct many of the tests, but they must set the standards for the test practices. Even if the testing is done by a separate product testing organization, the experience of the testers is critical.

A Design Margin Leads to a Robust Product Design

Words like "margin," "safety factors," and "safety zone" appear frequently in the design documentation for the successful technologies and products that we studied. Products with margin operate properly with parts whose dimensions are at their worst-case limits and in adverse environments. Margin generally does not occur by accident; rather, it is created by informed design decisions based on a thorough understanding of the product environment, use, and failure modes. "Designing beyond specification" and "redundancy" are two methods that can be used to provide design margin.

For example, the copier hot roll fuser shown in figure 5.3 operates in an operating space box surrounded by a safety factor region. This extra margin allows the copier to operate acceptably even if some unusual event (e.g., a temperature shift that causes the fuser to operate outside its normal temperature range) should occur. As the hardware is designed for the commercial version of the copier, the operating space must be designed into the new hardware. Special operating space tests must be run to verify that the operating space has been maintained. These quantified measures are used during the Product Design and Evaluation phase to assess the evolving product's ability to meet the PDS.

A tape cartridge library design team used the term "derating components" to describe their "conscious effort to ensure that all components . . . are effectively overdesigned for the job" [Barrett, 1987]. Components were overdesigned from 2 to 600 times the expected life of the product (even longer in a few cases), depending on how well engineers could predict loading conditions and other factors. The team also used redundancy to improve the product's reliability by installing a double-sided tape-handling gripper. If one gripper fails, the other can complete all required tasks, albeit at a slower rate than when both grippers are working.

Design Review

Concentration on a single project can lead to "tunnel vision," where the design team can no longer see certain problems because they are too close to the work [Barrett, 1987]. Design reviews solve this problem by serving as "the official second guess" for the product's design.

All of the studied projects used a design review as part of the development process. The design review often was performed by members of other related product teams. Even if no major problems are revealed during the design review, reviews are still useful because, in the words of a veteran engineer, "New people can successfully improve on old design, even *good* old design" [Galatha, 1988]. In many firms, design reviews are mandatory.

A Comprehensive Test Program

Most systems involve complex interactions among parts, assemblies, and the environment that cannot be modeled analytically. Thus, part, subassembly, and system testing are required to ensure that the product operates as desired under actual customer conditions. Testing was a prominent feature in all of the successful projects that we studied.

Parts, Subsystems, and System Testing

Component, subsystems, and system testing are among the longest and most expensive tasks in the development process. In the haste to reduce development time and costs, development leaders can be pressured to trim the test effort. In the studied cases, however, these development leaders required thorough characterization and verification of designs through testing. Corrective action times were reduced by having development teams test their own components and subassemblies. The structure and planning of the overall test program will be discussed later in this chapter in the section entitled Comprehensive Testing of the Product.

Operating Space Verification

One key requirement in the Product Design and Evaluation phase is to ensure that the product design operating space corresponds to the previously developed technology operating space. The mechanical aspects of the product are configuration sensitive, so when the hardware configuration changes the operating space must be verified again.

Performance confirmation may involve considerable effort. For example, thousands of inkjet printheads had to be produced to satisfy the characterization and reliability testing requirements for a commercial inkjet printer [Baker et al., 1988].

Deliberate Failure Evaluation

Tests to failure are imperative to verify sufficient design margin. For example, aircraft parts were scientifically destroyed to determine their margin in structural strength [Wilkerson, 1988]. However, it must be noted that prototype destruction is not necessarily called for; failure may be defined in many ways, including inadequate print quality (for a copier) or excessive signal loss (for a communications device). Failure mode prediction, evaluation, and effect analysis are key test-to-failure techniques.

Stress Testing

Stress testing is used selectively to ensure that the product will operate as expected when used by actual customers. For example, one firm tested its inkjet resistors at worst-case product overpower conditions [Baker et al., 1988]. When hot roll fuser engineers discovered that solid white and solid black zones caused the worst problems, copiers using the hot roll fuser were tested using both solid white and solid black sheets [Wilson, 1979].

Resistive ribbon systems in typewriters were evaluated using a "stress-pak" of papers; twenty types of paper that were very difficult to print on were run through the machine to ensure that quality type would be printed on all of the different papers [Voit, 1988]. An inkjet printer test subjected the product electronics to temperature cycles of 10°C per minute and to vibration levels that were four times higher than the product specification [Baker et al., 1988]. These tests were designed to attack serious, dominant failure modes that can be stimulated during normal product use. The results of stress testing require careful interpretation. When a failure occurs, it must be reported that "the product failed to meet these specific performance requirements under these specific conditions," not just that "the product failed." The implications of this mode of failure can then be interpreted in terms of customer use and plan developed to take the appropriate corrective action.

Effective Test Strategies

While some differences were noted across the case studies, all of the successful teams had a carefully defined and elaborated test strategy for their development efforts. One company stresses what it calls "early system integration," which entails the earliest possible build and test of a complete system [Hadden, 1986]. Another company's product teams have expressed a strong commitment to a "bottoms-up" approach, with parts tests leading to subassembly tests leading to system tests [Abbott, 1988]. Both methods, as well as combinations of methods, have proved effective when thorough design characterization was the goal. Of course, test strategy selection can be affected by the relative cost of the product. Additionally, early system testing is indicated when the product's subsystems are comprised of highly interactive technologies.

Labeled and Well-Known Critical Functional and Manufacturing Parameters

The discovery of critical variables was listed previously as an essential element for the Technology Selection and Development process. As the product is designed, the requirements for control of critical variables must be converted to subassembly functional requirements and then to parts design requirements.

In the successful case studies, these critical design decisions were well known to all members of the design team, including the manufacturing personnel.

One design element requiring improvement in even the successful cases is the description of critical product variables in the official product documentation. In many projects, the most valuable information about critical technology, design, and manufacturing factors resides only with the product team members, and is often hidden in engineering notebooks. The formal project documentation rarely denotes critical design dimensions, manufacturing controls, and related features that are needed for successful product manufacture. If the members of the original product team are no longer available (due to retirement, transfer, and the like), this information is lost. Later, if product or process changes are contemplated, the information has to be redeveloped, often at considerable cost, or "blind" choices are made, with possibly disastrous results. A solution to this problem will eliminate many product quality problems that currently appear during the manufacturing phase. (One simple method for denoting these critical items is presented in the Documents and Drawings Section that appears at the end of this chapter.)

The Product Design Specification

In his book *Total Design*, Stuart Pugh [1991] characterizes the PDS in great detail, based upon his work with Great Britain's Shared Experience in Engineering Design (SEED) program. We have adopted Pugh's categories, but we have organized them into six overall groupings:

1. *Product characteristics:* features, performance, product cost target, quality and reliability targets, aesthetics, ergonomics, size, weight, and modularization.
2. *Product life:* the product's life span, lives for replaceable parts or modules, warranty period, and storage or shelf life.
3. *Customer use:* installation procedures, documentation, maintenance, and disposal.

4. *Product development considerations:* development time (time risks), use environment, materials used (hazards), standards and safety, testing, company constraints (resources), and patents and legal ("local content").
5. *Manufacturing and product delivery considerations:* process selection, production volumes, product packaging, and product shipment.
6. *Market definition and plan:* customer identification, competitive assessment, market window (price, place, and promotion), market share and size.

The PDS spells out the complete requirements for the product to the product development team so that the parallel work in all the different areas will be compatible. The PDS is used by all involved in developing the product. It defines a framework for the work of the team. Since it affects all parts of the product development process, all relevant functional areas should participate in developing the PDS. In particular, the PDS categories should be considered as they apply to both the hardware and the software of the product.

Many product development groups are not accustomed to developing formal software specifications, but it is essential to do so. Regardless of form, the software portion of the PDS must include (1) all possible user inputs and outputs for both proper and improper use of the product, and (2) the mapping or transition from inputs to outputs.

Some PDS General Guidelines and Considerations

While it is important to have a comprehensive product design specification, it is equally important to have a concise one. If there are no limitations on the length of this document, it becomes so unwieldy that it is unusable. The best results come from having no more information than that called for in the categories. Some guidelines can assist in the format and control of a PDS. The initial PDS should be dated. Any amendments should be dated and identified. Each document revision is given a revision or issue number. The PDS should be written in a prescribed, structured format, not in essay form.

In developing the content of a PDS, one should be sure to:

- Define quantifiable targets for critical variables (or estimated values if these are unknown);
- Define the relative importance or tradeoff criteria for items that might conflict with each other;
- Resolve specification conflicts immediately, either by adjusting targets or by defining tradeoffs;
- Make sure that specification priorities agree with the customer benefits defined in the Final Product Definition and Project Targets phase; and
- Create one unified specification instead of splitting the document into separate engineering and marketing specifications.

The Initial Product Creation Process

Figure 7.3 shows the initial design creation effort. The major concepts to be considered in this effort are:

- Top-down design;
- Modular construction of the product;
- A "paper build" of the machine before parts are made;
- An internal design review prior to the first prototype build; and
- A bottom-up build and evaluation process.

Top-Down Design

External Considerations. The initial creation of the product configuration sets the stage for all subsequent design activity. Once the configuration of the product is established, the product design team has to live within the limitations set by this configuration. Once hundreds, if not thousands, of parts are designed for a specific configuration, the cost in both manpower and dollars to change the configuration is prohibitively expensive. Virtually all products have size constraints imposed upon them from the outside by the user. For example, if a laser printer is to be placed on someone's desk, its footprint is an important

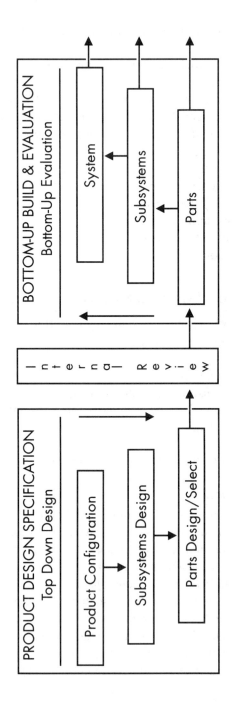

Figure 7.3. The initial product design step of the Product Design and Evaluation phase.

attribute to minimize, since desk space is so valuable. A small footprint is much more important than a minimum height to the top of the machine. Thus laser printers are likely to have footprint constraints upon their configurations. To follow this example a little further, many desks are pushed as close to a wall as possible. The user of a laser printer has to load paper frequently. Loading paper from the front of the machine is much easier than loading it from the back. Thus, a customer convenience-based external constraint on the configuration is that it should have a front-loading paper tray. A large number of external constraints on the configuration will exist after the user interface has been made most convenient and servicing needs are considered. In short, many important configuration constraints are external. Thus there is a need for top-down design (i.e., considering the external shape first as configurations are developed for consideration).

Internal Considerations.   Many functional considerations are affected by the space allowed inside the product for the functional parts. One must always provide enough internal space to accommodate the function reliably while the external configuration is being determined. The internal configuration of product also must be created by a top-down design process. Using the PDS, the partitioning of function into subsystems can be planned. This specification of subsystems and their interfaces constitutes the product configuration.

The complete high-level configurational design spells out (1) the flow of stimuli and responses among subsystems and (2) the flow of control among subsystems (e.g., sequential, alternative, iterative, concurrent). For example, a document being placed in the document feed tray of a copier is a stimulus, and the copier producing copies of the document and ejecting the document is the response. The sequential timing of the document feeder, the copier, the paper feeder, and the electrophotographic subsystems to produce the copies illustrates a flow of control among subsystems that must be designed carefully.

Mechanical, electrical, and control configurations must be defined to complete the top-level design. The integration of these subsystems is critical; today's digital electronic technology enables the engineer to dramatically improve the control of a machine. Machine-resident microprocessors can not only control the process timing but also can adjust the machine to specific environmental conditions, to record performance data, to diagnose problems, to recommend solutions, or to even call for service under certain conditions. Thus, the design team must consider what controls and features can be put under software control and take advantage of these capabilities during top-level design. Figure 7.4 illustrates this integration process that includes mechanical and electrical power transmission concepts, control concepts, and information strategies. At this point, various concepts of the machine will be investigated and the best one selected. This selection process is always a difficult task involving tradeoffs made with insufficient information. The selection of the best top-level design will anticipate the implications on the subsystem and subassembly design processes shown in figure 7.3.

Once subsystems have been fully specified, existing subsystems from other products may be considered for reuse in the new product. Candidate software and hardware subsystems must be both (1) well understood (i.e., clearly specified and implemented) and (2) good enough (i.e., sufficient for performance and reliability requirements) if they are to be used in the new product. There are enormous advantages as measured by cost and development time if previously developed and manufactured modules can be reused.

Controlled Iteration

The development of a product configuration is an iterative process that requires considerable discipline. Experienced engineers practice what is called "controlled iteration." That is, they deliberately create multiple configurations at this early stage and compare them over a limited time period.

This process is illustrated in figure 7.5. Several configuration concepts are developed from the PDS, each of whch requires a partitioning of requirements into subsystem modules. The competing concepts are then compared using a structured process. Many engineers use Pugh's configuration selection process, which pro-

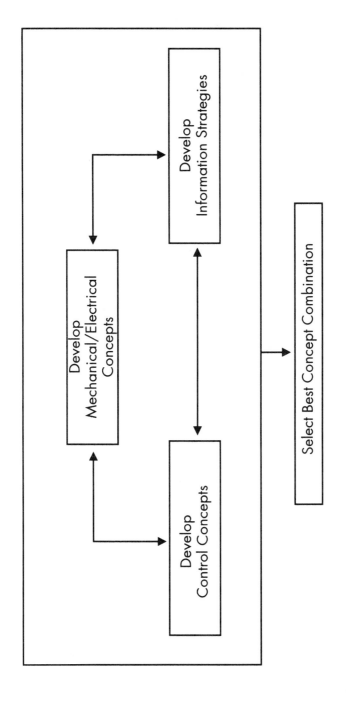

Figure 7.4. The integration of machine concepts.

vides a structured method for comparing various product configurations [Pugh, 1991]. Finally, the strongest designs are selected for additional development in the next iteration. This controlled iteration continues until the requirements are adequately met and the time limit is reached. The result is a design that is significantly better than the initial concept.

When the configuration development process is finished, the information displayed in figure 7.6 is available. This information includes the primary system configuration with physical groupings and module definitions, a product family definition with upgrade plans for expansion from a single product, and the subsystem configuration with the module interfaces defined.

The development of the configuration of a new machine has generally been practiced as an art. The most experienced mechanical designers usually develop the machine configuration under the supervision of engineers. Only recently have structured configurational design approaches been presented in the literature. In particular, Harrison [Wilson and Harrison, 1993] has developed a map of connections for representing complex machine configurations during the configuration development process. (Those interested in pursuring this fruitful area further should consult this reference.)

Subsystem Module Design and Parts Design

Physical System.   The next steps after the configuration design are the subsystems design and the parts design, as illustrated in figure 7.3. The subsystems are designed as modules, and the modules are composed of parts.

Software System.   A well-defined standard format for representing the software design should be used. Each design part should be traceable to its specification. During detailed design, the development team should ensure the quality of the design through a stepwise process of design followed by verification of design to specification. Ongoing peer review is essential to the management of software development.

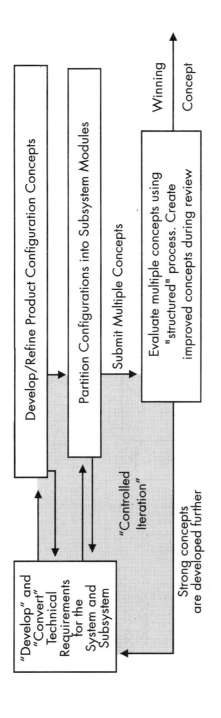

Figure 7.5. The product configuration stage within the initial product design.

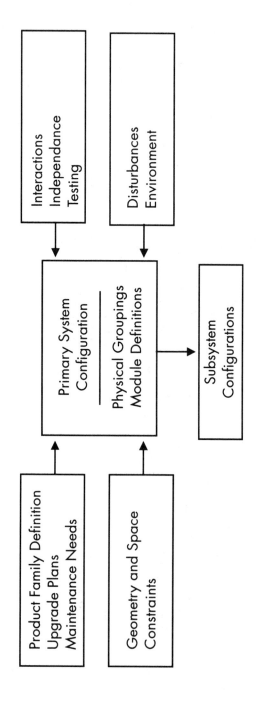

Figure 7.6. System and subsystem configurations.

Well-Designed Modular Configurations Enable Rapid Development

Well-conceived modular configurations that integrate hardware and software constraints and capabilities can greatly improve the ability of the project to be completed using a rapid development schedule. The team must make appropriate tradeoff decisions and divide functions between hardware and software controls. Putting the critical system variables under software control, for example, may make it easier to accommodate change during the development process.

To enable a rapid development schedule, the hardware configuration must avoid problems by:

- Accommodating critical locations and connections of modules;
- Minimizing the complexity of the mechanical and electrical connections; and
- Controlling the critical dimensions for robust functioning.

To enable a rapid development schedule, the software configuration must avoid problems by:

- Accommodating prototype configurations for early system testing;
- Having clearly defined interface requirements; and
- Developing structured, reusable modules.

Modular Construction

Subsystems are usually constructed as reusable modules in most competitive engineering organizations. Modular construction has become popular in the engineering of office machinery in the last fifteen years. (Figure 7.7 illustrates a modular machine configuration.) Prior to 1980, many machines were designed to have the minimum number of parts as a primary consideration in minimizing the cost of the machine. A comparison of the IBM Selectric typewriter and the IBM Proprinter shows the extremes of design philosophy exemplified by the absence of modularity in the Selectric to the snap-together modular design of the Proprinter.

Modular construction creates more parts since interfaces have to be constructed. But modular construction allows individual modules to be tested separately from the system, reused in derivative machines, and used as "field replaceable units" when service is needed. Independent testing speeds up the product design cycle, and easier replacement reduces service cost. The Hewlett-Packard laser printer has pioneered a process of replacing approximately one-third of its parts on a regular basis to eliminate the need for cleaning by service personnel. The cost of modular replacement is high, but the service personnel cost is virtually eliminated.

Software standards that support modular design are important for portability, reusability, and maintainability. Examples of basic standards for modular software design include:

- Isolating platform-dependent functions;
- Using ANSI standard implementation;
- Using parameters rather than global variables in modules;
- Ensuring readability through the consistent formatting;
- Ensuring understanding through the use of meaningful names for variables and symbolic constants; and
- Documenting the complete software architecture in a "call structure" (hierarchy of procedures) and all variables in a "data dictionary."

A "Paper Build" of the Product

The top-down design process ends with a paper or CAD-system build of the proposed configuration. The building of a machine on paper or with a computer prior to building it from its ultimate materials is a very important process.

The top-down design process proceeds through several drawings as the design is created. The first drawing is the "zero drawing," which contains just the allowable space for the total system, the allocated space for the modules, the location of the coordinate system from which all critical interfaces are measured, and the dimensions to the critical interfaces between modules. (The location of the origin of the coordinate system is called the datum from which all points are measured.) An extension

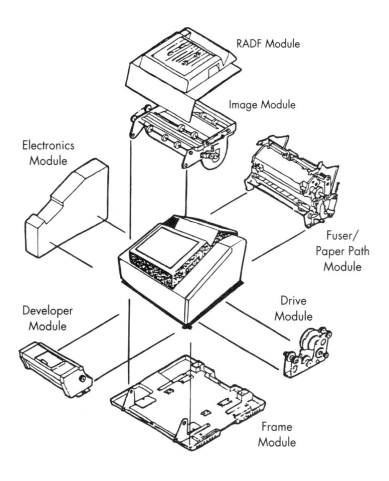

Figure 7.7. A modular copy machine configuration.

of the "zero drawing" is the "design layout," which is used to visualize and size the modules and parts being created. There can be design layouts of individual modules and design layouts of multiple modules as required by the design engineer. Of course, the lowest level of drawing is the individual part drawing.

Another very important layout that is used by disciplined design teams is the "machine control layout," which is constructed from the individual parts drawings as they are redrawn by their dimensions onto this layout. The process of redrawing the individual parts onto this layout constitutes a major part of the paper build of the machine. (CAD systems make this process much simpler.) Many errors and dimensional omissions can be caught as parts are placed on the machine control layout to check that they fit properly. Disciplined engineering teams require that the machine control layout be completed before the prototype parts are ordered. Engineers at Lexmark International, for example, have extended the concept of a geometric layout of the internal space to a functional layout that describes the measurement datums and allocation of space, the primary functional elements, and the media considerations (e.g., the paper path and paper behavior at interfaces, critical forces, velocities, dimensions, and so forth).

Internal Design Review

An internal design review (shown in figure 7.3) is held at the conclusion of the design process. Other engineers from within the organization bring experience from previous projects to bear on this project. The defense of the configuration can help clarify the design. If there are glaring weaknesses in the technology or configuration choices, they are likely to be caught in this review.

Some key items to be examined during the design review include:

- The control or functional layout (the paper build);
- The basic configuration for minimum complexity and adequate precision (examined using a map of connections) [Wilson and Harrison, 1993];

- The fit of the parts;
- A check of critical variables and dimensions to see if they are known and documented for control;
- A design that stays within the operating space of critical variables;
- A check of critical interfaces of software and hardware;
- A check of critical tolerances, function, and manufacturing capability to implement the critical dimensions;
- A check of critical timing of hardware and software (functional timing diagram);
- Memory and microprocessor speed calculations for throughput requirements;
- A software architecture review; a review of the plan for controlled iterations of tests; and
- The coordination of schedules for software and hardware.

Parts Ordering and Procurement

After the design review, the anxiously awaited parts procurement process is started. Parts ordering is expedited by having either an internal prototype capability or by having preselected suppliers make the parts. Multiple supplier bidding for prototype parts is a false economy, as development teams learned painfully during the 1970s. While purchasing groups were executing their business-as-usual three-bid process, some vendors were not even chosen within the first 3 weeks after the drawings were released and some parts were taking 12 weeks to procure. Competitive development organizations who moved the purchasing function into the product development team found that they could halve the usual procurement time of from 6 to 12 weeks for the procurement of complex parts; some teams were even faster. To execute a rapid development cycle, the development team should control the making and buying of parts and should not be dependent on outside functions.

Build and Preliminary Evaluation of Subsystems

The first level of preliminary evaluation shown in figure 7.3 is the checking of parts. The critical dimensions of these parts are

143

checked against the drawing requirements prior to starting the build of the prototype assemblies.

Fit Tests. Building the subsystem modules is the second level of evaluation for parts fit. The engineer assembles the unit or observes a technician doing the assembly while taking notes on all assembly difficulties. Experienced engineers pay much attention to solving fit problems immediately through firsthand knowledge of the problems encountered. Any interferences or very close fits call for a detailed tolerance study to ensure parts interchangeability on all subassemblies.

Initial Function Tests. The subassemblies or modules get the first level of functional testing if the subassemblies are truly independent modules. Often some additional operational support by special test rigs is required in order to demonstrate their function. These test fixtures are designed to allow critical functional tests to be run.

Wear and Life Tests. In addition to the initial functional tests, many life and wear studies are done at the module level in special test rigs developed just for this purpose. Extra units are built and tested in parallel. However, one should not order extra units for wear or life testing until the configuration is stable from the initial functional tests. Experienced engineers manage this part of the project very carefully in order to get critical life and wear test information early in the design and evaluation process. By getting this information early, weak areas may be identified and corrected prior to discovery of the problems during system testing.

The Build and Evaluation of the Total System

The third phase of evaluation is the build and evaluation of the total system. Often this first build is not of the total system but of the main engine only. It is important that the main engine function be demonstrated to work properly prior to the evaluation of ancillary functions. Thus the preliminary evaluation operation can proceed in an orderly fashion from the simplest machine to the more complex as the initial assembly problems are uncovered and solved.

For completely new products, it is not unusual for a corrective action cycle of redesign and rebuild based upon the solution of the initial build problems to be required. Good judgment on this decision is required. If the total system has too many initial function problems, comprehensive testing is futile, since the testing will provoke even more failures. Since too many failures at this stage will be confusing during evaluation, correction of initial function failures will be needed before proceeding with the comprehensive testing program.

After the initial function testing is complete, comprehensive system testing can start.

Comprehensive Testing of the Product

At the conclusion of the initial product creation effort and the preliminary evaluation, the comprehensive testing of the product is ready to start. Whereas the emphasis was on design during initial product creation, the emphasis is on evaluation in this phase. The evaluation process starts with the simplest set of functions of the product and expands to the total set of functions as the product is enhanced by its features. This process is an iterative evaluation process. The product evaluation process is illustrated in figure 7.8.

The first step is the definition of a comprehensive test plan by using the requirements of the PDS. At this point, it is critical to analyze the product's potential failure modes and the conditions that will cause the worst effects of the failure. These failure modes must be tested.

Whereas the initial function testing during the design evaluation process is "testing for success" and ensuring that the machine can function properly, the next part of the testing program is "testing for failure." This testing program is a bottom-up effort that starts with parts evaluation, moves to subsystem evaluation, and then continues with system evaluation, as shown in figure 7.9. This program is also a controlled iteration process of testing to failure, taking corrective design action, and

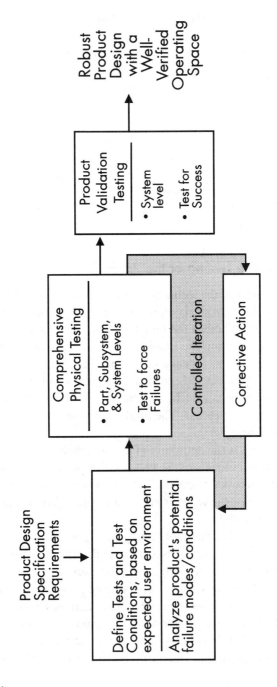

Figure 7.8. The product evaluation and corrective action step.

retesting as shown in figure 7.8. The final step is product validation testing, which is a system-level test for success. Completing this comprehensive design and evaluation process results in a robust product with a well-verified operating space. A more detailed discussion of this evaluation process follows.

Planning the Comprehensive Evaluation Process Using Controlled Iteration

Even the foregoing brief discussion conveys the complexity of the evaluation process. Thus it is necessary to plan the evaluation process carefully to prevent it from becoming chaotic as the team struggles to both provoke failures and eliminate them by redesign.

The concept of "controlled iteration" serves well at this point in the development process, just as it did in the configuration selection process. An example of controlled iteration during the evaluation process is the conducting of multiple tests over a planned period while scheduling the updates of hardware and software into the system tests by the calendar. Planned redesign updates to the system allow a systematic improvement of the machine while deliberately refraining from incorporating incomplete solutions of problems into the machine. The plan also includes adding function to the product from the minimal configuration to the most fully featured configuration.

This comprehensive test planning includes tests being conducted in succession at the parts, subsystem, and system levels. For example, a four-month schedule of system testing may have planned updates at the end of each of the first three months followed by the final tests for success in the last month. Planning and executing such a comprehensive test plan take a great deal of cooperation within the team to ensure that the problems are identified and solutions demonstrated. As new problems surface, considerable flexibility is required to solve them as well as to stay on the controlled iteration schedule. The integrity of the design and evaluation team is called to task in this process. There is no substitute for experienced design and evaluation engineers to ensure the success of this very difficult and critical process.

A final requirement for a successful evaluation and corrective redesign program is a detailed problem tracking log that

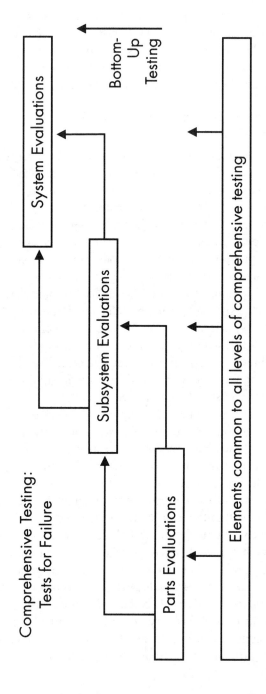

Figure 7.9. The product testing process.

states the problem, the root causes, the solution, and the confirmation testing. Team management should be focused on the successful execution of this process, rather than on making presentations to management and/or corporate staff personnel. Most successful new product development teams have autonomy within the team with the responsibility to meet function, cost, and schedule resting with the team leader. (Xerox uses the chief engineer as this autonomous leader.)

Figure 7.8 is a summary of the product evaluation and corrective action process just discussed. Note that failure mode and effect analysis is an analytical technique used prior to comprehensive testing. This method identifies the modes of failure that have the most harmful effects and thus helps prioritize the product design process and the comprehensive testing plan to ensure that these modes of failure are blocked by the product design.

Within the comprehensive testing effort shown in figure 7.9, four major types of testing are performed:

- Stress testing, to provoke failures and determine design margin;
- Life testing, to understand and to plan the replacement of any life-limited parts;
- Testing to specification, to assure that everything works right within the operating environment specified; and
- Operating space verification, to ensure that the critical variables are controlled within necessary limits.

Testing for Failure

Testing for failure is a very important testing concept, but one that can be easily be misapplied. Experienced engineers know that there are many failures in every new design. The task is to discover these failures and correct them as soon as possible during the product design and evaluation efforts. Testing for failure is a stress testing method used to provoke the failures. Once revealed, the engineering investigation proceeds to the root cause of the failures and corrects them in a redesign process.

Testing for success is an obvious thing to do. "Just test the product as the customer will use it and solve all the problems that occur," an inexperienced engineer might say. Even an experienced engineer might suggest to "just submit the product to the Product Test organization and solve the problems they uncover." Both of these statements have some merit, but each can result in a noncompetitive product development process. Testing for success will eventually reveal the problems that need to be solved, but only after a very long testing period. In testing for success, one never knows just how close failures are to the test region. Thus a product may be tested successfully in a test laboratory environment but may fail in a factory or customer environment that is only slightly out of the laboratory test range.

There is a specific set of failure modes "hidden" in any machine or system. Some people describe the process of finding these failures as "peeling the onion" – finding a layer of problems and solving them to peel back another layer to solve more problems. Each layer has a smaller and smaller probability of occurring in the customer environment. One finally stops when the problem layer corresponds to a negligible probability of occurrence. Other phrases used to describe these methods include "provoking failures" and "force it to fail and fix it."

Efficient stress testing requires considerable judgment and experience, especially when determining what constitutes a negligible problem for the customer population. For example, only a tiny fraction of automobile users will require reliable ignition at $-100°F$. Designing for this requirement would delay the announcement of a new model several months and add significant cost to all vehicles – not a reasonable tradeoff. A design engineer must make these decisions with the assistance of others on the team. Only design engineers are in the position to say how much delay and cost are required to meet an increasingly difficult requirement, and they should thus be major decision makers in these situations.

The stress testing method is also used to find the operating space of the critical variables that control the process. By discovering the limits of the operating space and redesigning to enlarge it, the engineer builds design margin or robustness into the product. The experienced modern engineer uses statistical design of experiments or Taguchi Methods® to test the limits of an operating space. Designed experiments simultaneously vary several critical variables beyond their normal limits to investigate the operating space. This investigation is a repeat of the operating space tests made during the Technology Selection and Development stage, but this time the machine hardware is representative of a production process. Much has been written about experimental design, but very little is taught in most engineering schools. Some references [Peace, 1993; Diamond, 1981] are given at the end of the chapter to guide the reader. The testing method to be used repeatedly in the comprehensive testing phase illustrated in figure 7.9 is the testing for failure method.

Parts Evaluations

Failure testing for parts primarily provokes wear and breakage types of failures. Highly stressed areas must be analyzed to quantify the magnitude of the stress but also must be tested to failure to ascertain the margin of safety that exists. Experienced engineers know that wear rates are a sensitive function of friction and the lubrication conditions and may vary by an order of magnitude depending upon these conditions. Thus, a large safety margin is necessary to guarantee a robust design that is not sensitive to environmental or machine condition changes. Processes such as case hardening, in which wear resistance and life are a function both of the hardness level and case depth, must be verified as adequate for the part application. The safety margin of the breakage mode of failure for critically loaded parts must also be verified by appropriate fatigue tests to ensure that the parts will not fail in the field.

Testing of Modular Subsystems

Modular subsystems make it possible to test several components at once in a stressed situation. For example, electronic circuit boards are stress tested by Hewlett-Packard using a test method called "strife" testing. This involves exciting the boards mechanically with a random excitation over a comprehensive frequency range while systematically raising the temperature of the environment. Thus the electronic components are stressed by the cause of their predominant mode of failure (abnormal temperature) while the soldered connections are mechanically stressed by the induced vibration. As the failures occur, weak areas are redesigned or reprocessed to eliminate the modes of failure at that level of stress. This method creates a margin of safety by solving problems that exist outside the normal operating ranges.

Mechanical subsystems can also be stressed in this manner since the mechanical connections are often a source of reliability problems. Fasteners are subject to loosening, and lubrication and strength of elastomer parts are affected by temperature.

Another important use of modular subsystem tests is determining the life span of "life-limited" parts. For example, some parts in machines that move paper (such as elastomer rollers) are subject to abrasion and must be replaced at specific intervals. Similarly, belts must be replaced at intervals in belt-driven machines. Astute engineers do not specify machines to run to failure but will specify replacement prior to failure based upon appropriate testing. In new machines, this testing is usually accomplished most conveniently by system testing.

The old adage, "If it ain't broke, don't fix it," is not appropriate in a competitive environment where customers demand ultrareliable machines. Any failures that cannot be designed out of the product must be prevented by a program of parts replacement at specified usage intervals so that the product does not fail and interrupt the customer's work. Dramatic examples of this preventive approach are the Canon copier and Hewlett-Packard laser printer, in which the electrophotographic unit is designed as a module and is completely replaced when the unit runs out of toner. This module constitutes approximately one-third of the machine's parts. The parts are all still functional, but the new module replaces all of the parts of the machine that will later deteriorate because of toner contamination. This module replacement eliminates the need for a service person to correct contamination-related failures (the major failure mode of electrophotographic machines) and allows the customer to make a simple replacement. The machine copy quality is virtually guaranteed not to deteriorate by this process and the expense of service personnel is dramatically reduced. This preventive modular replacement process has been proven successful through customer experience. Most small laser printers now follow this practice.

System Testing

While subsystem and parts testing are occurring in parallel to answer the life-limiting questions, system tests are run to answer environment-related questions. These stress tests are designed to find the operating space relative to the external environment that is to be experienced in the customer application. Temperature and humidity are two environmental factors that are often critical. For example, all internal combustion engines intended for automobiles, buses, or trucks must be tested across extremes of temperature and humidity. To this day, diesel engines are dramatically less robust relative to starting in low temperatures than are gasoline engines.

All paper-handling machines (such as copiers, laser printers, and offset presses) must also be tested throughout a range of temperature and humidity. Hot and wet conditions (e.g., 90°F and 80-percent relative humidity) cause paper to become very limp and hard to handle. Thin papers (such as 16-pound papers) can become unreliable in such an environment. Cold and dry conditions (e.g., 60°F and 8-percent relative humidity) create another mode of failure – electrostatic charging of the paper. Paper can become attracted to itself and ground planes, thus creating electrostatic force fields that have to be identified and eliminated. Testing to identify these failure modes has to be done at the system level.

Figure 7.8 also shows that the PDS feeds information into the subsequent blocks of analysis and evaluation. The expected usage environment describes the conditions under which the machine will be used. For example, the machine may be expected to perform continuously 24 hours per day, or it may be used intermittently during a 24-hour period with no more than 30 minutes of continuous operation. The usage characterization is very important since it determines the requirements for internal cooling of a machine, which in turn determines space requirements and noise level.

The effects of variation of a moving medium such as paper must be tested at the system level if the medium moves through several subsystems. Reliability requirements for many products are so high now (for example, one paper transport failure per 10,000 sheets fed through a laser printer) that the failure analysis must be done by imagining the mode of failure and then exaggerating it in stress tests to assess what may need to be redesigned to handle extreme conditions without failure. The interfaces of modules, where paper sheets are handed off from one set of guides and rolls to another, are the most frequent sources of paper-handling problems. The guides will often be designed (or redesigned) to handle a sheet with a folded corner or front edge and then tested with sheets with folded corners to see if the paper handling has improved over the previous design. Again, stress testing is the way to provoke failures as quickly as possible.

Electronic boards, particularly those that contain memory devices, must be shielded from electrostatic discharge and electromagnetic fields. Both these types of tests must be done at the system level even though they may have been done at the board level because the machine itself may generate these environments. Thus temperature, humidity, and electrostatic and electromagnetic fields are all examples of environmental conditions that must be tested at the system level.

Summary

The documents and drawings listed below constitute the work products of the product design and evaluation process. Completion of these documents is usually tied to major checkpoints of the process. Disciplined engineering teams ensure that this documentation is complete and correct and make a point of building on this information for future products as "lessons learned."

- The *product design specification* describes all the functions required of the product in technical terms.
- The *module technical specifications* provide the module technical requirements for hardware and software.
- The *project schedule* identifies key events (e.g., completion of the product design specification, the design review, and controlled iteration schedule).
- The *business plan* (created in the Final Product Definition phase and updated in this phase) defines target costs and volumes determine net profit.
- The *zero drawing of configuration* includes datums plus the outside physical envelope of the product.
- The *machine control layout* defines spatial relationships among modules, envelopes and interfaces, and some parts.
- The *functional layout* defines critical functional variables and their operating space.
- The *module layout* defines module designs and some parts.
- The *parts drawings* provide complete information for manufacture of parts.
- The *bill of material* specifies the number and the cost of parts.
- *The comprehensive test plan* describes tests for failure tests and tests for success.
- The *software design records* include high-level specification and design; detailed specification and design; the module call hierarchy; a data dictionary; and the source code.
- Failure and engineering change records document product modifications.
- The *final report* details the theory of operation (how the product is supposed to work technically), the final performance results (the product's actual performance versus the functional requirements), and the key technical problems and recommended corrective action.

In the 1970s and early 1980s, many US engineering organizations produced drawings and specifications that were "thrown over the wall" to manufacturing. In newly competitive engineering organizations, the manufacturing people are on the team, so there is no "wall." The manufacturing members of the team use this information to ensure the production of robust products using controlled processes.

The responsibility of the team usually extends through the first six months of manufacturing and delivery to the customer thus creating a major shift in the attitudes and performance of the development engineers. The engineers who have developed the product feel a responsibility to ensure the delivery of the product they designed to the customer and not to just deliver documentation to the manufacturing organization. This extension of the responsibility of the development team is a major reason why the model of product development featured in this book is superior to the practices of the 1970s and 1980s. In the succeeding chapters, we will follow the model from the engineering and evaluation activities to the manufacturing and customer delivery activities to see how they are integrated.

References

Abbott, Tom (1988), "Improving the Product Development Process," notes from ASME short course, "Case Studies of Engineering and Manufacturing Methods for Superior Results," Atlanta, GA, April 18 – 19, 1988.

Baker, J. P., et al. (1988), "Design and Development of a Color Thermal Inkjet Print Cartridge," *Hewlett-Packard Journal*, August 1988, pp. 6 – 15.

Barrett, David (1987), "Designing for Reliability," working paper from course ME 597, "Investigations of Design Methodology for Superior Products," at the University of Colorado at Boulder, April 22, 1987.

Galatha, Matthew (1988), "Design for Automation – The IBM Proprinter," notes from lecture at the University of Tennessee, Knoxville, TN, April 14, 1988.

Hadden, L. Lyndon (1986), "Product Development at Xerox: Meeting the Competitive Challenge," notes from presentation to Copying and Duplicating Industry Conference, February 10 – 12, 1986.

Peace, Glen Stuart (1993), *Taguchi Methods®: A Hands-On Approach*, Addison-Wesley, Reading, MA.

Pugh, Stuart (1991), *Total Design: Integrated Methods For Successful Product Engineering*, Wokingham, England: Addison-Wesley, 1991.

Voit, W. (1988), "Resistive Ribbon Technology," notes from case study presented at the University of Tennessee, Knoxville, TN, April 14, 1988.

Wilkerson, H. J. (1988), "Boeing 747 Testing," notes from lecture at the University of Tennessee, Knoxville, TN, April 12, 1988.

Wilson, Clement C. (1979), "A New Fuser Technology for Electrophotographic Printing Machines," *Journal of Applied Photographic Engineering*, Summer 1979, pp. 148 – 156.

Wilson, Clement C., and Kunlé Harrison (1993), "Comparing Configurations of Complex Machines Using the Map of Mechanical Connections," *Proceedings of International Conference on Engineering Design (ICED) 93 (Vol. 1)*, The Hague (Netherlands), August 1993, pp. 83 – 92.

Selected Bibliography

Diamond, Bill (1981), *Practical Experiment Designs for Engineers and Scientists*, Van Nostrand Reinhold, New York.

157

CHAPTER 8

MARKETING AND
DISTRIBUTION PREPARATION

Superior product design is not a sufficient condition for product success. Customers must be made aware of the product and then must be provided with some method for purchasing and obtaining the product. The Marketing and Distribution Preparation phase, highlighted in figure 8.1, occurs in parallel with the Product and Manufacturing Process Design phases so that the product can be introduced to its market in a timely fashion.

A complete guide to marketing and distribution planning is beyond the scope of this book. Therefore, this chapter provides only an overview of some key aspects of this phase.

Milestone Goals

The milestone goal for the Marketing and Distribution Preparation phase is *to design and prepare marketing, distribution, and customer support systems that reflect and enhance the product's value to the customer.* If a product is distinctive for its luxury, these systems should dignify the product accordingly. If a product is distinctive for its advanced technology, these systems should reflect technical substance. If a product is distinctive for its competitive price, the selection of channels should be based on their effectiveness and economy. The customer's exposure to marketing and distribution systems for the product should reinforce the particular values that the product represents and provides.

Process Description

Marketing-related issues are often categorized within the "4 Ps" of marketing: product, price, place, and promotion. These interdependent factors, shown in figure 8.2, take on varying degrees

160

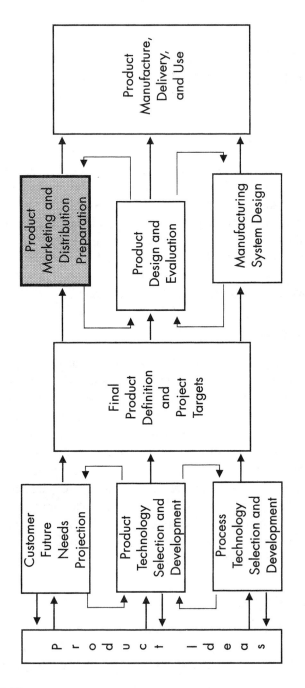

Figure 8.1. The Product Marketing and Distribution Preparation phase within the overall product development process.

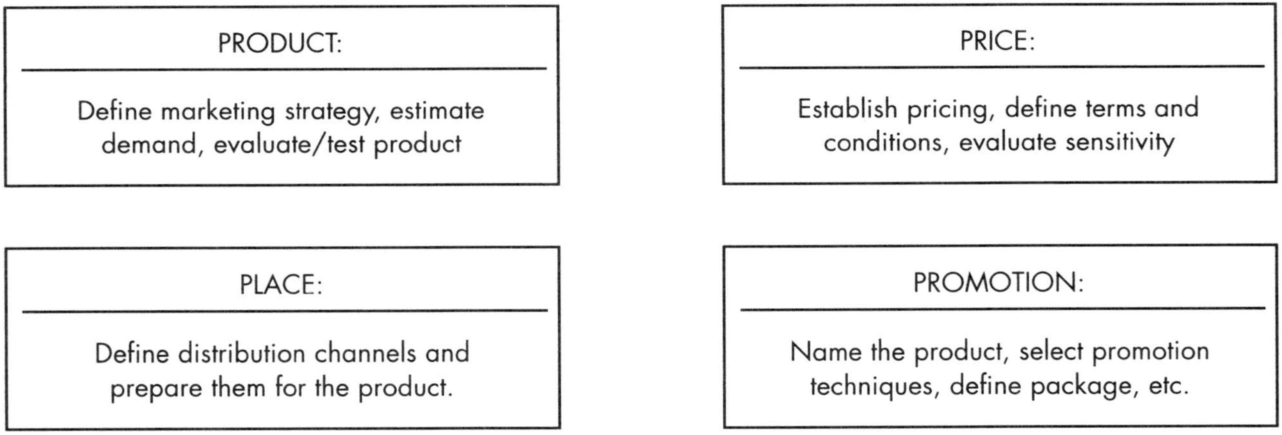

PRODUCT:

Define marketing strategy, estimate demand, evaluate/test product

PRICE:

Establish pricing, define terms and conditions, evaluate sensitivity

PLACE:

Define distribution channels and prepare them for the product.

PROMOTION:

Name the product, select promotion techniques, define package, etc.

Figure 8.2. The Product Marketing and Distribution Preparation phase.

161

of emphasis depending on the specific product and the nature of its market. The resources and effort needed to address each of these four categories can also vary dramatically across types of products. While they may seek the counsel and assistance of outside groups, successful product development teams pay attention to their new product marketing and generally do not delegate these major decisions (either intentionally or by default) to others.

A Complete Product

The "complete product" may include not only the physical product itself, but also a number of additional customer benefits, such as a warranty, service plan, spare parts, or other defined support. Defined product options must be made available, the product must be delivered to customers, and it may have to be installed by expert personnel. In some markets, these complementary or auxiliary services, rather than the product itself, are what differentiate the product from its competitors. Examples of services that can increase product value include:

- Fast delivery;
- Free installation;
- Free maintenance;
- Toll-free ordering;
- Easy-to-use, complete documentation;
- Built-in tutorial or operating instructions;
- On-site training;
- Ready technical support; and
- Application customization assistance.

Customers purchase products for their benefits, not simply for their features. For many products, benefits and value can be enhanced greatly by providing (either with the product itself or for additional fees) these additional services and support. On the other hand, the expense of such "extras" can cause a new product to be overpriced if the additional efforts are not needed or appropriately valued by customers.

A Strategic Price

Product pricing can provide tremendous leverage for achieving market and financial success with the new product. In this phase, the team has the opportunity to evaluate what pricing considerations can be used to improve the sales and profitability for the new product. While the fundamental product price *has already been determined* (within the income projections contained in the business targets), there may yet be considerable discretion as to how that net price is obtained.

A firm must understand how pricing is structured in its marketing channels (discussed in the next section) so that the business targets are based on expected actual receipts. Those not directly involved in new product marketing sometimes forget that the firm does *not* receive the product's full retail price unless it sells the product directly to customers. Retailer markups or salesperson commissions can account for as much as 20 to 50 percent (or more) of the product price paid by the end customer! The firm's estimated income from the product, then, must account for these differentials.

Another key point is that the product does not necessarily have to be sold at one price only. If the product uses multiple sales or distribution channels, it may be appropriate for the product to be sold at different prices in those channels. Preferred customers might be offered preferred pricing programs. Standard orders might be priced lower than a product combination that requires customization. Combinations of factors may be used to set prices – airlines charge different fares, for example, depending on the class of service, whether or not the ticket is purchased in advance, and the demand for the particular flight.

Products and their associated services (if any) can be combined with pricing to affect product sales and income. Software programs, for example, can be "bundled" to sell for less than what the individual packages would if purchased separately. Conversely, products and services can be "unbundled" and priced separately. For example, users who can install a product themselves might be offered a different price than customers who require extra services.

Incentives and discounts can play an important role in stimulating demand for, and managing the cash flow from, a product. Volume discounts can be used to encourage higher quantity purchases. Discounts may be provided to "fast payers" to reflect savings generated from not having to finance the product's purchase. Rebates might be offered based on the dollar amount or the quantity of purchase over some time period. Price discounts may be given to dealers that feature the product in their advertising.

Another general issue that often arises is whether the product should be assigned a manufacturer's suggested retail price, or MSRP. The MSRP may or may not be a serious measure of the price ordinarily paid for the product in the market. Ballpoint pens, for example, are often sold by retailers at the MSRP. Automobiles, on the other hand, are rarely purchased at their sticker price. MSRPs sometimes are set artificially high from what is expected to be the "real" purchase price to give customers the psychological impression that they have gotten a good deal by buying at an apparent discount.

Some firms may offer customer financing for product purchases by extending credit to customers at or above the market rate (depending on the risk). When run well, the firm can profit from both the product sale and from the loan made to finance that sale. Alternatively, the firm may extend below-market financing to promote sales by reducing customer cost. Under extended terms, a customer might not have to pay for a specified period of time. The firm, in effect, provides a product discount by paying the interest associated with financing the delay. While promoting sales, each of these options has an associated cost. The relative costs and benefits to the firm and the customer must be assessed.

A leasing option may be appropriate for high-priced products that require customers to make significant investments. A leasing option reduces the customer's initial cost, making it easier for the customer to afford the product. Examples of products that are now commonly leased are cars, computers, copiers, building space, and land. Alternatively, the firm may arrange to sell the product to leasing companies, who then assume the responsibility (and risk) involved in using a leasing program.

An Accessible and Value-Added Place

"Place" refers to how the product actually reaches the final customer, both in terms of its purchase and in its delivery. The term "market channel" is often used to describe the process of how and where customers purchase the product and how the product physically travels from the firm to the customer. *The success of many innovative products can sometimes greatly depend on the selection (or alternatively, the development) of appropriate market channels.* Innovative new products sometimes need innovative new market channels!

For example, the IBM PC was successful (at least in part) because it avoided the high costs of the traditional market channel for computers – the direct sales force. The PC team's pursuit and development of less costly computer retail channels allowed the PC to be sold at a price consistent with its objective of providing a low-cost, personal computing alternative. The idea of selling computers to customers through retail stores instead of through highly specialized, company-based sales personnel was the innovative marketing method needed to support the innovative product. Since that time, of course, the development of even less costly direct mail and discount warehouse channels has made many of these early computer retail channels obsolete.

Market channels are generally evaluated in terms of their accessibility, cost, and the added value they offer to the customer. Accessibility involves both "reach" (the visibility to the customer) and ease of use (the convenience to the customer). Costs incurred in the channel may be absorbed by the firm or may be passed on to the customer. For example, the firm may choose to include UPS shipping fees in the price of its product or may charge an additional shipping fee when the product is purchased. In any case, the channel's impact on product costs and price must be evaluated.

A market channel also can be used to provide the additional

value and services related to the complete product and to assist in the product's promotion. A market channel, for example, may:

- Help customers install or setup the product;
- Enable the customer to review the product before buying;
- Enable customers to obtain the product immediately; or
- Facilitate warranty repairs and replacements.

Depending on the specific product, it may be desirable to use multiple market channels for selling and distributing the product.

The product "place" encompasses a number of logistical factors as well. Ordering, handling inquiries, following up on sales leads, providing support, and collecting payment are all systems to be planned and prepared in this phase. Depending on the newness and the requirements of the selected market channel, the product may or may not be able to take advantage of the firm's existing processes for these activities.

Well-Targeted Promotion

The critical factor in developing product promotion is to ensure that it is consistent with the product definition and market targets established in the Final Product Definition and Project Targets phase. Mass media are expensive; the firm's objective should be to choose promotion media that reach the highest number of target customers at the lowest cost. Promotion should be squarely aimed at the product's target customers, using the product's defined "points of difference" as key elements of the campaign. If the product is to have superior ergonomic features, for example, promotional materials need to highlight that superiority.

As with distribution channels, the reach, cost, and added value of prospective promotional activities must be evaluated. An advertising agency or consultant may be needed to assist in the development of the program if the firm does not have its own expertise.

The strategic scheduling of the product's introduction to

166

market, the training of sales representatives, and the preparation of promotional materials are key activities in promotion planning. These activities are often carried out through resources outside the product development team, but the management of these activities is best done within the team. It is important that the firm resist the temptation to announce the new product too early, before it is clear that the product can be completed successfully and on schedule. Excessive pressure to meet an unrealistically early ship date can lead to skipped development steps and unreliable products.

Summary

The Marketing and Distribution Preparation phase of product development requires extensive planning of product, price, place, and promotion. Innumerable decisions are involved to ensure the introduction of a complete product at a strategic price, in an accessible and value-added place, and with well-targeted promotion.

At the conclusion of this phase:

- Value-additions have been defined and prepared;
- A pricing strategy has been established, including price of auxiliary services;
- Market channels have been defined and are ready to receive the product; and
- Product introduction and promotion have been planned and are ready for implementation.

An overview of the key aspects of marketing and distribution planning have been provided in this chapter. References are suggested for the reader who wants further details on this phase of product development.

Selected Bibliography

Duerr, Michael G. (1986), *The Commercial Development Of New Products*, The Conference Board, Washington, DC.

Kuczmarski, Thomas (1988), *Managing New Products*, Prentice-Hall, Englewood Cliffs, NJ.

Small Business Administration (1991), *Marketing for Small Business: An Overview,* Washington, DC.

Wizenburg, Larry (ed.), (1986), *The New Products Handbook*, Dow-Jones Irwin.

CHAPTER 9

MANUFACTURING SYSTEM DESIGN

The Manufacturing System Design phase of the product development process, highlighted in figure 9.1, initiates the planning and construction of the manufacturing processes needed to produce the new product. Effective product development organizations take this phase seriously, for the activities within this phase are integral to achieving the cost effectiveness and reliability of both the manufacturing processes and the product itself. Manufacturing system preparation requires a thorough knowledge of the product, the firm's manufacturing processes, and other manufacturing processes that may be available from other firms. Thus, the team needs knowledgeable manufacturing engineers to execute this phase properly. The effort needed varies widely, depending upon the type of product. If the product is a new platform requiring new production facilities, much planning and implementation will be needed. If the product is a close derivative to one already in production, a much smaller effort is needed to convert the manufacturing facility so that it can produce the new product.

Close observation of figure 9.1 shows that the Manufacturing System Design phase is displaced slightly to the right from the Product Design and Evaluation phase. This deliberate displacement signifies that the product's design *must be complete and stable* before the manufacturing system design can be completed. While much product and process design may be performed concurrently, the process design must always lag slightly *behind* the product design.

Since the early 1980s, numerous books have been written about "new" US manufacturing methods developed in response to the superior performance of many Japanese manufacturing firms. Many American manufacturers struggled to learn why as much as one-third of their manufacturing costs were spent on

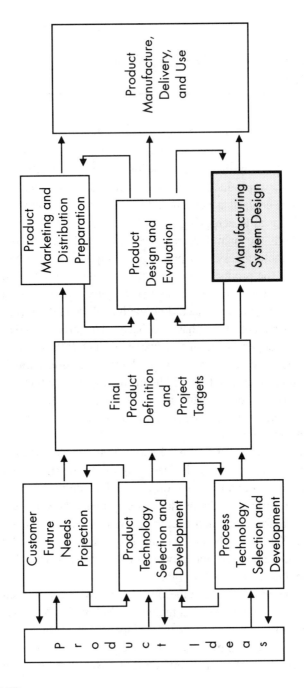

Figure 9.1. The Manufacturing System Design phase within the overall product development process.

disposing of and fixing defective products ("scrap and rework") and why Japanese firms did not appear to have this same problem. These US manufacturers were slow to realize these Japanese manufacturers had been implementing manufacturing improvement programs such as continuous improvement and worker empowerment efforts for over 20 years. The "new" flexible manufacturing, lean manufacturing, and just-in-time (JIT) manufacturing techniques currently in vogue throughout US manufacturing are primarily derived from the well-established Toyota Production System and the experiences of Fuji Xerox. Because both of these clearly superior manufacturing systems are well documented elsewhere, they are not described in this chapter.

Instead, we describe the *preventive methods* that can be used to eliminate the major manufacturing system problems that cause much of the engineering and manufacturing rework observed in many US factories. In particular, we show how to connect the critical variables controlling the functional performance of the *product* to the critical variables that control the *manufacturing process*. In other words, we relate the product's *engineering tolerances* to the *capability and control* of their manufacturing processes. Using this technique to select and control the manufacturing process for the product prevents the one-of-a-kind problems that still plague many American manufacturing firms and reduces the incidence of major product recalls caused by manufacturing variation.

Milestone Goal

The milestone goal for the Manufacturing System Design phase is *to select and construct cost-effective, capable manufacturing processes for parts manufacture and product assembly.* These processes are selected carefully to ensure that they can reliably create the critical features that determine the product's functional performance. Critical processes are identified as such and are usually controlled by the firm for maximum process quality control.

The term "cost effective" is used within the milestone goal to emphasize that the process generating the least total cost is to be used, not just the process that yields the lowest parts or manufacturing costs. This total cost accounts for not only the cost of operating the process but also for the costs generated from the variation within the process. Thus, a more-expensive, higher precision process may indeed be more cost effective than a less-expensive process if the higher precision lowers overall costs by reducing the number of defective parts produced, by limiting the loss of product reliability caused by variations in manufacturing, and/or by making it easier to control the process.

Process Description

An overview of the Manufacturing System Design phase is illustrated in figure 9.2. The first task (item 1) requires that the team define its production strategy. The production strategy must be defined early enough relative to the Product Design and Evaluation phase so that the product design can be made compatible with appropriate manufacturing methods. The production strategy does just that: it matches the product design with the manufacturing process design.

As shown in item 2 in figure 9.2, the production processes to be used are determined and their capabilities assessed. Item 3 shows the design and construction of manufacturing equipment, the layout of this equipment on the factory floor, and the development of setups and tests needed along with the equipment. Item 5 shows how items 2 and 3 interact with the design of the product. These items are also affected by the selection and management of the parts suppliers shown in item 6.

Finally, a manufacturing system design review (shown in step 4) is held to ensure that all processes are capable, that suitable process controls are in place, and that the process design is compatible with the product design. For maximum effectiveness, the design review includes appropriately selected members from both inside and outside the team.

In this chapter, we will largely concentrate on the efforts to determine production processes and assess capability (shown in item 2) of this phase.

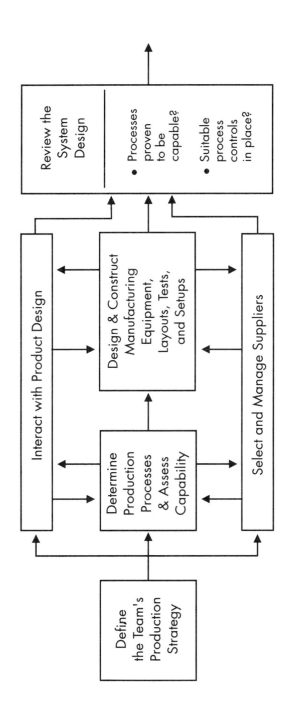

Figure 9.2. The Manufacturing System Design phase.

Essential Elements

The essential elements for the Manufacturing System Design phase are:

- Processes are restricted to those that are well defined and characterized.
- Critical dependencies are identified. Any parts or assembly processes that would have serious consequences if they are disrupted are identified. The critical variables and conditions of these processes are identified and closely monitored.
- Critical processes are performed and controlled internally or through especially close relationships with reliable suppliers.
- Suppliers are selected based on their capabilities (including cost), not just on cost alone.
- Automation is attempted only after the process is simplified and its stability is proven.
- Processes (particularly automated processes) have designed in features to either prohibit errors or to detect errors automatically.

Restricted, Well-Defined, and Characterized Processes

Appropriate process technology development in the Process Technology Selection and Development phase is a critical prerequisite for achieving this essential element. The imperative behind this essential element has been described best by the engineers who stated, "Use standard, well understood processes. Historically, when we have strayed from this concept we have suffered low yields, cost increases, and many engineer hours of process support and characterization" [Baker et al., 1988].

Critical Dependencies Identified

Any event, condition, or other process factor that could cause serious system development or production disruptions is identified in advance. These process "dependencies" (the critical variables and conditions upon which these processes depend) are identified early so that the manufacturing system can be designed to monitor and control them.

Alternative production methods are developed when necessary and made available to minimize the number of critical dependencies. Then, if a dependency creates a problem the team has an action plan ready.

Critical Manufacturing Processes Performed Internally

In the successful cases that we studied, processes related to the manufacture of critical technology or design parameters were controlled internally by the firm itself or else were controlled very closely with preferred (usually single-source) suppliers. For example, the hot roll for a copier was manufactured in-house to ensure control of critical material, thickness, and other parameters affecting the performance of that roll within the copier [Wilson, 1979]. A printer team developed proprietary, in-house processes to ensure that all print quality standards would be met during product manufacture.

Supplier Selection Based on Capability, Not Just on Low Bids

While sensitive to parts cost, the successful firms that we studied placed more emphasis on process capability during their supplier selection efforts. One firm studied their injection-molding and stamped-parts suppliers and selected only the most capable as single-source suppliers for specific products. These suppliers also participate during the parts design for new products. Suppliers are required to supply error-free parts (no defective parts are permitted) and often must submit their process quality control documentation with the components that they ship. Many of the larger firms also help their smaller suppliers develop the process quality controls needed until that supplier becomes able to produce error-free parts.

Automation Allowed Only After Processes Are Stable

In successful projects, the automation of processes was performed *after* the critical manufacturing processes were demonstrated successfully using manual procedures. This essential element was so important to one product development team that they included the warning, "Don't automate until feasibility is proven" in their development phase goals [McLeod et al., 1989]. Another team tested the feasibility of their automated processes by modeling those processes in a special laboratory. Only after the automated process was demonstrated successfully in that lab could it be installed on the production line [Deaton].

If automation is pursued before manufacturing processes are stable, subsequent changes to the process may force the team to redesign or scrap the automation equipment. Substantial changes in automation programming and/or equipment may be necessary if the early automation development is no longer compatible with the revised process.

Another consideration is the effect that designing for automated assembly has on the ability to assemble the product manually. For example, IBM automated the entire assembly of its Proprinter, which became famous for being so easy to assemble. The printer's layered, snap-together design used no screws and was designed specifically for robotic assembly. However, when production was moved to another facility, robotic assembly of the Proprinter was abandoned. It was so easy and so fast to assemble the printer by hand that the benefits from automated assembly were not worth the costs to move the equipment to the new location and to assume its associated capital costs.

Another project, an IBM disk drive product, again demonstrated that designing a product for automated assembly often eliminates the need for that automation. The simple assembly operations remaining after improving the design made manual assembly much less expensive and more flexible. Unfortunately, as in the Proprinter case, the diskette team committed to purchasing the automation equipment at the start of the project only to discover that its use in assembling the product added little value and created much expense.

GM also made huge investments in automation, particularly in robots, based on what it assumed would be its productivity benefits. Critics of this multibillion dollar program suggest that GM selected unreliable and unproven automation technologies that did not function properly when installed. Many of these automation investments were also used to "solve the wrong problem." For example, expensive robotic vehicles were installed to move parts inventories, but these efforts did not alleviate the real problem, which was that there was too much inventory in the plants [*The Economist*, 1991]. These experiences, and many others like them, demonstrate that automation efforts must be approached very carefully if a team is to extract the benefits from that investment.

Processes Have Designed-In Features to Prohibit or Detect Errors Automatically

Experienced process designers use process design guidelines just as product designers use product design guidelines. One of the most important guidelines to follow when developing a process (particularly an automated process) is that each step within the process should be checked to ensure that the step was done properly. The overall process then can be thought of as a series of "step, check, step, check." Any item failing a check is discarded, either at that station or at another assembly station downstream. By building in error detection and correction capability, the process can yield a defect-free product. Process checks are particularly critical for high-speed processes to preclude the high-speed production of defective products. An automated assembly process that uses process-error-detection methods has the potential for being more reliable than manual assembly, which is always subject to variations in personnel, training, and so forth. This potential suggests that the primary reasons for automating any process should be to improve reliability and quality, not just productivity.

The Manufacturing System Design Effort: Implementing the Milestone Goal

We have already noted that the milestone goal for this phase is to select and construct cost-effective, capable manufacturing processes for parts manufacture and assembly. *The key step for achieving this goal is to select manufacturing processes based on their "process capability."*

The Selection of Manufacturing Processes

Figure 9.3 shows the method for selecting production processes and evaluating their capability. This method must be performed for each process that is to be used in manufacturing every part and building every assembly. The first step is to assess the requirements that need to be met by any process that might be selected (i.e., what the process must achieve to guarantee the function of the part or assembly). The second and third steps are to identify process candidates and to evaluate them against product function, cost, and other appropriate criteria. Candidates are also assessed for their ability to produce with little variation relative to the product's functional requirements. (See item 4 in figure 9.3.) Finally, the process that best meets the functional criteria and process capability requirements is selected.

Assessing the Capability of a Process to Meet Critical Requirements

In many development efforts, there is a continuing struggle between the product engineers and manufacturing engineers over whether product specifications are "too tight" or processes are "too loose." One very important lesson from our case studies is that firms who compete successfully in world markets *pay a great deal of attention to the match between product requirements and process capability*. In particular, they are quite adept at improving the ability of their processes to produce products with very little variation. Many Japanese firms, for example, limit the permitted variation of their processes so strictly that many US engineers are inclined to conclude the product is overdesigned and the manufacturing specifications unreasonably stringent. They might argue that such precision is unaffordable. However, this level of precision *is* affordable if by doing so the firm eliminates potential scrap and rework.

How is the capability of a process determined? Figure 9.4 illustrates the four-step process for assessing and improving process capability.

Step 1: Ascertain the product's critical requirements. To begin, team engineers must recall which product requirements

PERFORM FOR EACH PART/ASSEMBLY:

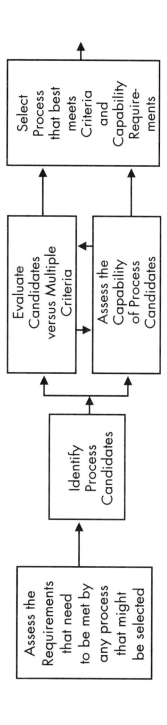

Figure 9.3. The selection of manufacturing processes.

179

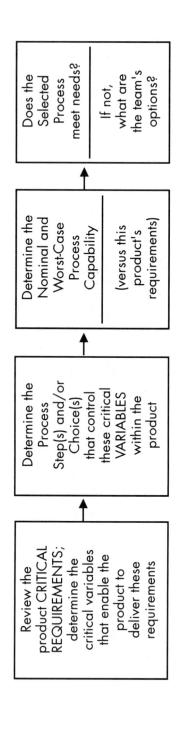

Figure 9.4. The process for determining process capability.

are critical for achieving customer satisfaction. These are the features, performance, and quality attributes that contribute significantly to the product's value. The product design specification (PDS) provides a good overall guide for understanding which requirements are critical. Additionally, the team needs to identify what methods can be used for *measuring* these characteristics; these may have been developed during the Technology Selection and Development phase or while writing the final product definition or the PDS.

For example, the "touch" of the keys on a computer keyboard is a critical customer requirement when the computer is used for word processing. One keyboard manufacturer with years of experience in designing typewriter keyboards determined the force versus displacement profile of the keystroke for "best touch." This profile is specified in the PDS for the keyboard. A test device was then designed to measure the force-displacement characteristics of the keyboards.

Next, the *critical variables* that enable the product to achieve the critical functional requirements are determined. These critical variables may be particular components, part dimensions, surface finishes, or certain assembly relationships between parts. In the keyboard example, the force versus displacement profile (the critical function) is controlled by the spring constant and free length of the spring, by several dimensions of a pivot lever, and by the flatness and squareness of the keyboard guide plate. Each of these critical variables is specified carefully so that the keys have the desired force-displacement characteristic. Tolerances (the allowable ranges) are established for these variables so that the desired touch can be achieved over the entire range of tolerances that occur. Through this method, engineers ensure that the desired customer function (touch) is always achieved through control of the product's critical variables. By controlling the critical variables, the team can assure that the product always remains within its operating space. It is through this conversion that technical information is communicated from the Technology Selection and Development phase into the Manufacturing phase.

Step 2: Determine the process steps that control the critical variables. Once the critical features (i.e., critical dimensions, surface finishes, and so forth) of the parts or assembly are understood, the team then determines which step (or steps) in the manufacturing process is responsible for the creation of that feature. More than one process step for a part may be needed to create some features, and others may be dependent of the specific characteristics of several different parts. If so, all of the steps need to be assessed using this procedure.

Step 3: Determine the process capability versus the product's requirements. Comparing the process capability to the product's requirements is the most difficult step of this process. The problem is exacerbated by general shortcomings in both engineering education and in the firm's management of its manufacturing facilities. Many US-educated design engineers are never instructed in process capability and control as part of their academic work. So when they design parts, the design engineers set tolerances on those parts without knowing whether the manufacturing process that will be used to make those parts will be capable of producing to the specified accuracy. On the other hand, manufacturing engineers are often trained to select the cheapest manufacturing process that just "meets the specs"; then their employers base their performance evaluations on their ability to achieve the lowest parts costs. These shortcomings set the stage for the constant design-engineer-versus-manufacturing-engineer struggle mentioned earlier. (Calculating the process capability is so important to the selection of the right process that we present it in the next section.)

Step 4: Determine whether the selected process meets design needs. Once the process capability is determined, the team must decide whether the process is appropriate for this particular part or assembly. Again, this step is so significant that we discuss issues related to the decision in another section.

Computing Process Capability

Figures 9.5 through 9.10 show visually how to determine the relationship between the product's engineering specifications and the ability of a process.

Figure 9.5 shows the design target with its accompanying

specification limits. The target value for each critical variable is retrieved from product design information. Next, the allowable tolerance, which establishes how much the variable may vary from its target value, sets the lower specification limit (LSL) and the upper specification limit (USL). These limits, in conjunction with the target value, define the total range of permitted variation for the critical variable. The limits and tolerances must be set so that the product will function properly so long as the critical variable is anywhere within this range. While in figure 9.5 the LSL and USL are equally spaced from the target value, they do not necessarily have to be. The key is to set these values so that the critical variable can vary while the product still "works right."

Figure 9.6 illustrates the variation that occurs in any manufacturing process. The process mean and six standard deviations (6σ) of variation about that mean are shown. The process mean and standard deviation values are computed from the statistical process control (SPC) data that the firm should collect for all of its critical production processes. In general, a "normal" distribution can be assumed, but only after a firm has demonstrated that the process is in control.

Once specification limits (see figure 9.5) and variation of the process (see figure 9.6) are known, these ranges can be compared, as shown in figure 9.7. After centering the manufacturing process onto the design's target value, the process capability can be computed from its "capability index" (Cp). As shown, Cp is the quotient of the allowable tolerance range divided by the six standard deviation range of the corresponding manufacturing process.

Figure 9.8 shows that capable processes maintain a Cp of at least 4/3. (Note that we assume that the process mean is centered on the target value.) A study of figure 9.7 and the use of algebra show that a Cp of 4/3 allows the process mean to vary as much as one standard deviation either way from the target value before the (6σ) range reaches either specification limit.

Some very aggressive firms require that their process Cps equal or exceed 2.0. Processes that attain this very high level of capability make it possible for the process mean to move as much as three standard deviations (3σ) either way before the 6σ process

184

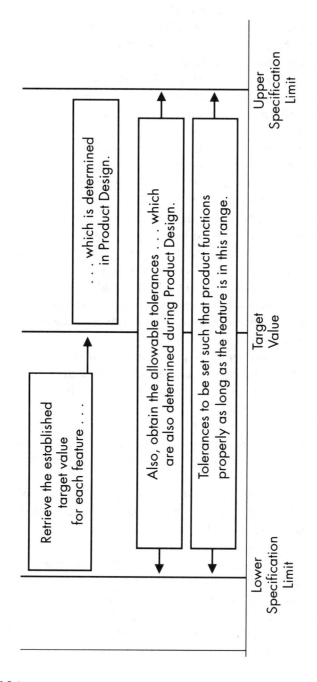

Figure 9.5. Establishing the target value and assigning tolerances.

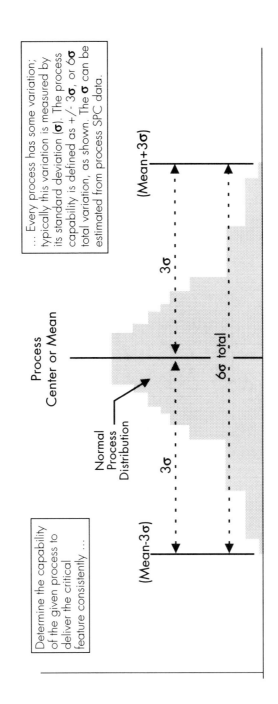

Figure 9.6. Manufacturing process variation.

186

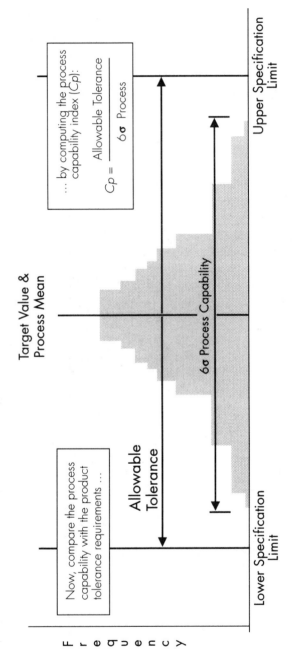

Figure 9.7. Determining the process capability index (*Cp*) by comparing the process variation to the design tolerance requirements.

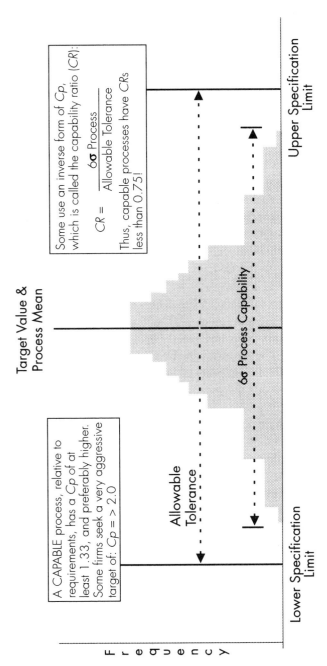

Figure 9.8. Determining whether a process is capable or not from the capability index and/or the capability ratio.

variation range reaches either specification limit. The ability to allow the process mean to move 3σ each way, or 6σ total, is the basis for the so-called "six sigma" programs that have been highly publicized by firms such as Motorola. There are legitimate arguments that this is an unreasonable and unnecessary goal for mechanical parts. Some companies are finding that a Cp of 5/3 is adequate for the manufacturing processes for mechanical parts.

Of course, even the best process may not be able to maintain its process mean exactly on the design target value. Figure 9.9 shows how to compute process capability when the process mean is off-center from the target value. The capability measure Cpk is computed as the ratio of the distance of the process mean to the closest specification limit divided by half of the normal 6σ process variation (equal to 3σ). In this example, the process mean has shifted toward the USL so that the numerator of the ratio is based on the USL. If the process mean is closer to the LSL, then the LSL is used.

The criteria for using Cpk to decide whether or not a process is capable is shown in figure 9.10. When Cpk equals 1.0, the 3σ process variation limit lies exactly on a specification limit. (In figure 9.10, it would overlay the USL.) If the process Cpk can be improved to 4/3, the 3σ process variation limit moves one standard deviation inside the specification limit. Aggressive firms that achieve a Cpk of 1.5 have a process with a 3σ limit that is a full 1.5 times the standard deviation inside the closest specification limit.

Process capability decisions are relatively simple once the company has determined the values of Cp and Cpk that it needs to use (provided that they choose physically realizable values). As illustrated in figure 9.11, a process may be used if it meets or exceeds the Cp and Cpk requirements. If one or both criteria are not adequately met, the team generally must pursue one of four options. It must either improve the process that was selected so that it can meet the requirements, select another process that is more capable of meeting the requirements, change the tolerances, or invoke "coping" methods.

The most obvious solution for a process capability problem is to reduce the process variation, as shown in figure 9.12. By reducing the process variation, both Cp and Cpk are increased.

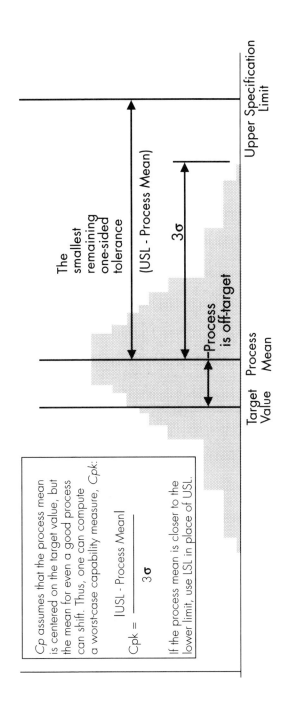

Figure 9.9. Determining whether a process is "capable," when the process has an "off-center" mean.

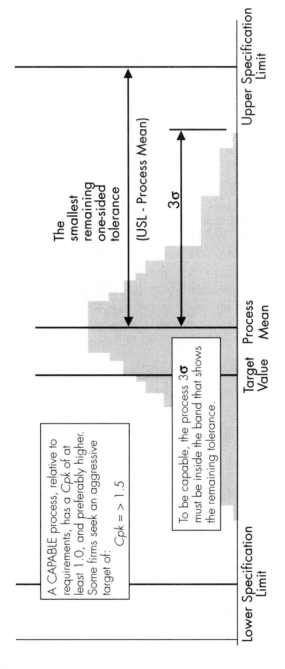

The smallest remaining one-sided tolerance

(USL - Process Mean)

3σ

A CAPABLE process, relative to requirements, has a Cpk of at least 1.0, and preferably higher. Some firms seek an aggressive target of:

$Cpk => 1.5$

To be capable, the process 3σ must be inside the band that shows the remaining tolerance.

Lower Specification Limit

Target Value

Process Mean

Upper Specification Limit

Figure 9.10. Manufacturing process variation.

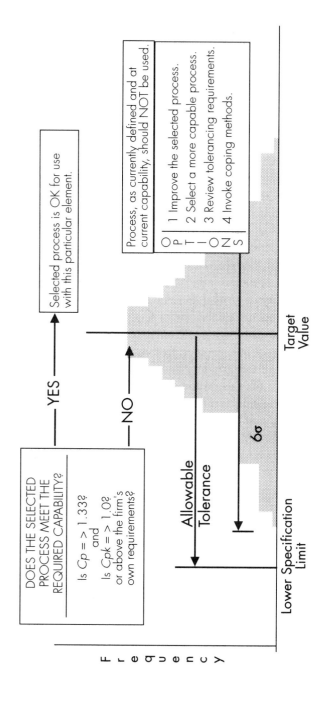

Figure 9.11. Determining whether a process is appropriate for use in an application; if it is not, assessing the available options.

191

If just the *Cpk* is inadequate, the process capability (as reflected by *Cpk*) can be improved by improving the ability to adjust or set the process mean to keep it at the target value.

Process capability can also be improved (see figure 9.13) by substituting a more capable process; that is, by using a process which has less variation (i.e., a smaller 6σ value). Using a more capable process is one method used extensively by Japanese copier and laser printer firms. An example of this method is to consider how manufacturing processes are selected for the small shafts (usually about 1/4 inch or 6 mm in diameter) that are used throughout these products. If selection is based on parts manufacturing costs, one might choose to use cold-rolled steel shaft, which then must be plated to provide corrosion resistance. The cold-rolled method creates shafts with diametral tolerances on the order of 0.005 inch plus an additional tolerance of 0.001 inch for plating. Instead, these Japanese firms greatly reduce the process variation in forming the shaft diameter by choosing to use a ground and polished stainless steel shaft, which can be made to a tolerance of less than 0.0005 inch and requires no additional plating tolerance.

The extra precision obtained from using a more expensive stainless steel and the grinding and polishing processes obviously costs more than using the plated cold-rolled steel shaft. However, the precision of the grinding and polishing operations and the elimination of the plating operation create a dramatically higher process capability. This improved capability (obtained through reduced manufacturing variation) eliminates the potential for undesirable interferences that can occur as the shafts are inserted through bearings. By selecting a very capable process, the Japanese firms eliminate the costs of scrap and rework caused by shafts and bearings that fit improperly.

When process improvements are impractical or uneconomical, the tolerance that was set for the target value may be reviewed. A review may indicate that the tolerance was set too stringently to enable capable manufacturing. An obvious response is to expand the tolerance range enough to accommodate the process variation (see figure 9.14). Before attempting this, however, the team must evaluate fully and comprehensively the effect of the change to ensure that the tolerances are not extended

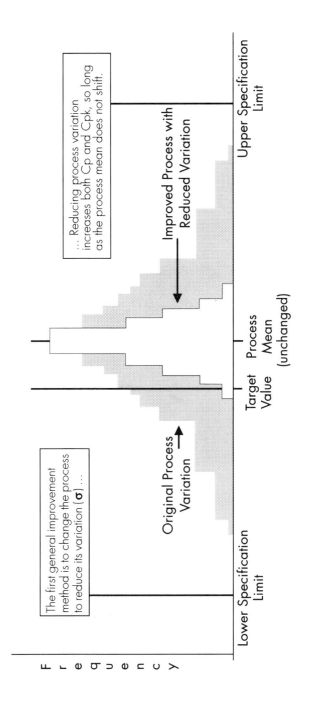

Figure 9.12. Improving a process by reducing its variation.

The first general improvement method is to change the process to reduce its variation (σ) ...

... Reducing process variation increases both Cp and Cpk, so long as the process mean does not shift.

Improved Process with Reduced Variation

Original Process Variation

Upper Specification Limit

Lower Specification Limit

Process Mean (unchanged)

Target Value

Frequency

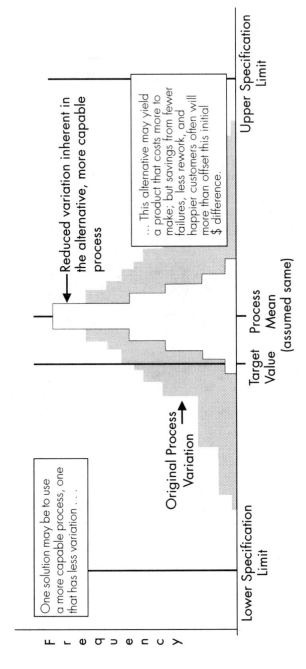

Figure 9.13. Improving process capability by selecting a more capable process that has less variation.

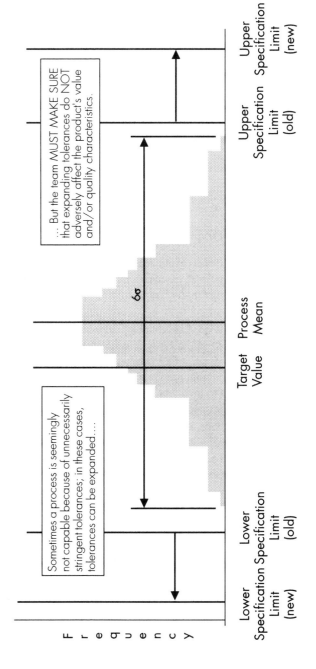

Figure 9.14. Improving process capability by increasing allowable tolerances. This option is allowed after the team demonstrates that the increased tolerances do not harm the product's value or robustness.

195

into a region where the product will fail to function properly. Industrial history is full of cases where the unwise expansion of tolerances has caused widespread product failures in the field. Teams must resist the urge to solve manufacturing problems by expanding tolerances, since these "solutions" can easily create their own, often much more expensive, customer problems.

When a process cannot be matched to tolerance specifications so that the selected process can be capable, various coping methods may be considered. Some common approaches and examples of their use are provided in table 9.1.

Table 9.1. Coping strategies that can be used when a process cannot be made capable enough.

Method/Strategy	Description/Contents/Example
Inspection (100%)	Inspect feature on every part produced. If feature is a part dimension, measure dimension on every part made. Use parts within tolerance. Scrap or rework those outside tolerance.
Sorting	Inspect each and sort into usable groups. (Example: electrical resistors are measured and sorted into ±1-percent, ±5-percent, and ±10-percent groups.)
Matched assembly	Group mating parts to achieve desired assembly characteristics. (Example: use the larger balls in the bearing race assemblies which have the larger clearances.)
Full-function and stress testing	Fully test the function controlled by this feature to ensure that the feature is not defective. Must test every product during or after manufacturing. Can be expensive, but sometimes can be combined with planned manufacturing testing.
Design redundancy	Provide product with more than one way for achieving the required function that is controlled by this feature. (Example: Motorola put two identical circuits on one ultra-high-density μ processor because they could not make a 100-percent-defect-free chip. Chip functions even if one circuit fails.

Formal Identification of the Critical Variables and "Critical to" Designations

Once the critical variables and their allowable tolerance ranges are determined so that the product can meet its performance requirements, there is a critical next action that is not standard practice in many US firms. This action is *to formally identify these critical variables on the engineering drawings and specifications for the product!* This differentiation of the critical dimensions and features on the drawings from the multitude of other items that also appear is critical information that needs to be communicated to the manufacturing process and its people.

Table 9.2 illustrates a formal system for identifying three types of critical variables: critical-to-function, critical-to-assembly, and critical-to-manufacture. These identifiers are used to distinguish the few critically important dimensions and specifications from the many others that appear. By placing these identifiers on important dimensions, specifications, and so forth, there is no doubt about what the critical

Table 9.2. "Critical-to" designation symbols. These symbols are used to indicate which features and variables are critical to the value and robustness of the product.

Symbol	Critical to	Description
<CTF>	Function	Item is directly related to the ability of the part or assembly to function and deliver its customer requirements.
<CTA>	Assembly	Item does not directly affect function but does affect the ability to assemble other items that do.
<CTM>	Manufacture	Item does not affect function but does affect other processes, dimensions, or manufacturing setups that do affect function.

variables are. When combined with engineering change control of the drawings and specifications so that changes cannot be made without due consideration, the "critical-to" indicators can anchor an effective process control system.

The use of the "critical-to" indicators is illustrated in figure 9.15. These designations should be used on all engineering drawings and specifications. If the part is provided by suppliers, these suppliers must be instructed in their meaning. In general, all critical features should be verified through the use of statistical process control (SPC) of the manufacturing processes that create those features.

The importance of this type of quality control (and the strength of its enforcement) must not be underestimated. One case study team established an identification scheme similar to the one described here. To protect the quality of the product in manufacturing, any part or assembly that is found to be out of specification with respect to any feature marked "critical" may not be used without the approval of the top-level manufacturing site manager. We highly recommend that firms make this critical-variable identification method part of their standard engineering design and manufacturing practices.

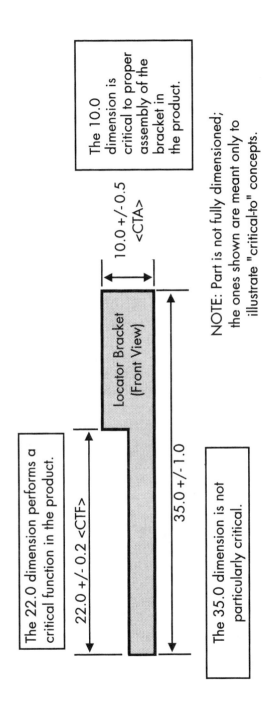

The 10.0 dimension is critical to proper assembly of the bracket in the product.

10.0 +/- 0.5 <CTA>

Locator Bracket (Front View)

35.0 +/- 1.0

NOTE: Part is not fully dimensioned; the ones shown are meant only to illustrate "critical-to" concepts.

The 22.0 dimension performs a critical function in the product.

22.0 +/- 0.2 <CTF>

The 35.0 dimension is not particularly critical.

Figure 9.15. Example of the use of "critical-to" designations.

199

Summary

Successful completion of the Manufacturing System Design Phase results in:

- A comprehensive plan for how all parts and assemblies will be produced using capable manufacturing processes (for both in-house and supplier-provided items);
- A list of critical dependencies with an action plan for overcoming each dependency;
- The formal identification of all critical variables on all relevant engineering drawings and specifications;
- A plan for the design and construction of the manufacturing equipment;
- The actual design and construction of the manufacturing equipment;
- The selection and qualification of all suppliers; and
- The successful completion of a manufacturing system design review.

The successful completion of the Manufacturing System Design phase depends significantly on how well the manufacturing system designers and product designers can work together. As a Texas Instruments manager [Randall, 1990] said, *"Our biggest problem . . . is the isolation of design engineering and manufacturing engineering or process engineering (from each other)."* Once again, the team effort that is needed throughout the product development process is also particularly important within this phase.

Additionally, the problems that many manufacturers face have been compounded by their overall lack of knowledge of modern process control methods. Individual firms – and entire industries – have had to mount enormous (and expensive) educational efforts to train their manufacturing process and product development personnel in process control methods. Many firms also have had to bear large costs to train their own parts suppliers. It is past time for the universities to assume this educational task, so that their engineering graduates will have an understanding of modern process control before they join industry.

The process capability methods that we discuss in this chapter are taken from the references listed in the following section.

References

Baker, J. P., et al. (1988), "Design and Development of a Color Thermal Inkjet Print Cartridge," *Hewlett-Packard Journal*, August 1988, pp. 6 – 15.

Deaton, F., et al., "The (ProPrinter) Story," IBM Corporation, Charlotte, NC.

McLeod, G., et al. (1989), Interviews with members of the Hewlett-Packard Plotter Pen and Paintjet teams, San Diego, CA, May 1989.

Randall, Ron (1990), personal correspondence.

Wilson, Clement C. (1979), "A New Fuser Technology for Electro-photographic Printing Machines," *Journal of Applied Photographic Engineering*, Summer 1979, pp. 148 – 156.

The Economist (1991), "Rusting Away: America's Car Industry," London, August 3, 1991, pp. 64 – 65 (no author cited).

Selected Bibliography

IBM, The Quality Institute (1984), *Process Control, Capability, and Improvement*, IBM Corporation, Thornwood, NY.

Texas Instruments Defense Systems and Electronics Group (1992), *Malcolm Baldridge Application Summary*, Dallas, TX. (This TI group won the 1992 Baldridge National Quality Award.)

Wilson, Clement C., and Michael E. Kennedy (1989), "Quantification of Critical Product Characteristics," ASME Winter Annual Meeting, San Francisco, December 1989.

CHAPTER 10

PRODUCT MANUFACTURE, DELIVERY, AND USE

The Product Manufacture, Delivery, and Use phase, highlighted in figure 10.1, is the "ultimate" phase within the product development process. Only if the team is able to manufacture and deliver a product that pleases customers with its performance and satisfies their value needs can there be a successful completion of the product development process. The competitive need to shorten the product development process and to improve product quality makes this phase critical to the timely introduction of superior products. When this phase is part of an effort to develop a technically complex product, what occurs here is the culmination of hundreds of person years of work, the efforts of hundreds of people, and expenditures of perhaps millions of dollars.

Milestone Goals

All the major milestone goals for the Product Manufacture, Delivery, and Use phase relate to the *demonstration* of the ability to manufacture, assemble, and deliver a quality product in a cost-effective manner, consistent with actual customer demand for the product. (This phase often lasts through the first six months of production under the control of the product development team to ensure that all the objectives are met.) Process control methods are applied to critical processes to limit manufacturing variation and to ensure product reliability and quality. Processes are improved – not just maintained – by the manufacturing team as a continuing effort. Process improvements repeatedly decrease the amount of scrap and rework produced, thus yielding repeated process cost reductions. Potential customers are reached effectively by the marketing channels such that the product demand targets are met. Product delivery

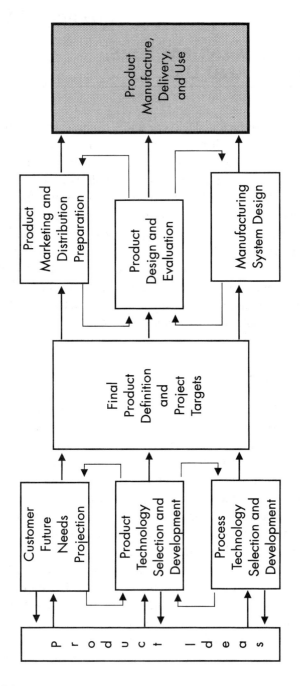

Figure 10.1. The Product Manufacture, Delivery, and Use phase within the overall product development process.

is provided in a timely fashion as promised and without damaging the product. Customers are prepared adequately in the use of the product so that they are delighted with their product investment. The quality of the delivered product is evaluated and rapid remedial action is taken to correct any product or process problems that occur. The milestone goals that reflect that all these actions have been taken successfully are to:

- Pass the pilot run testing program to ensure that all manufacturing processes are performing as required;
- Pass the product launch readiness review to ensure that all manufacturing, delivery, marketing, and service processes are ready for the launch;
- Complete the product infant mortality tracking and appropriate corrective actions to ensure all unexpected failures are corrected immediately and root causes are found to protect the product's reputation with the customer;
- Ensure that continuing improvement programs are working effectively for all processes (i.e., that proper objectives and measurements are determined);
- Ensure that all target income and expense items in the business case are being met and that corrective action is taken regarding exceptions;
- Recycle the product development team to initiate more new programs leaving only a small support team after six months.

Process Description

As shown in figure 10.1, this phase receives information from three major phases: the Marketing and Distribution Preparation phase, the Product Design and Evaluation phase, and the Manufacturing System Design phase. Figure 10.2 shows the major events within the Product Manufacture, Delivery, and Use phase.

The first full trial of the manufacturing facility occurs as part of the pilot manufacture step (item 2 in figure 10.2). Products are produced using the actual production process and then the process is stopped. Both the processes and the products produced

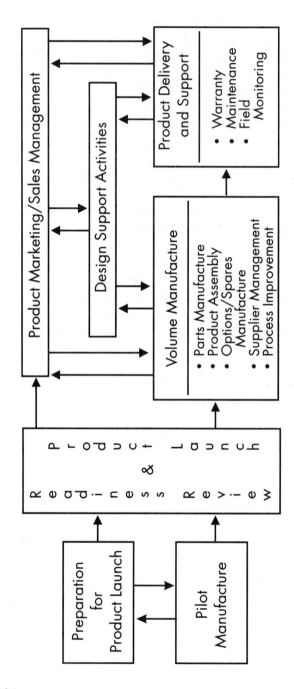

Figure 10.2. The Product Manufacture, Delivery, and Use phase.

are evaluated as shown in figure 10.3. Corrective action is taken on all process and product problems that must be corrected for product launch.

Readiness for Launch and Product Launch

Readiness for product launch is ascertained by a review of the readiness of the converging phases of marketing, product design, and manufacturing and delivery. This process is illustrated in figure 10.4. After the readiness review is passed successfully, the product is announced. Some firms announce prior to having the product available for sale and others have the product universally available when the announcement is made. That is, items 3 and 4 in figure 10.4 are reversed in some cases. Item 5, infant mortality tracking, is a crucial program for new, complex products. All performance failures and service calls are reported to engineering for analysis. All broken parts are returned to the factory for engineering analysis or engineers are dispatched to the field to analyze the root causes of failure and to determine immediate corrective action. This program is discussed in a separate section later in the chapter.

Volume Manufacturing

After corrective action has been taken on problems found during pilot production, volume manufacturing is restarted, as indicated on both figure 10.4 and figure 10.5. The product manufacturing activities shown in figure 10.5 are divided into parts manufacturing and subsystem and system assembly. Many firms now use outside suppliers to perform the majority of parts manufacturing and complete the subsystem and system assembly in-house.

Controlling the quality of incoming parts is a critical activity that drives the quality of assembled units. During the 1970s, the number of parts suppliers used by US firms grew seemingly without bounds as firms attempted to reduce cost by moving their parts manufacturing to outside suppliers and by using their purchasing department's to bid suppliers against each other. The quality programs (zero defect and the like) that were invoked by

208

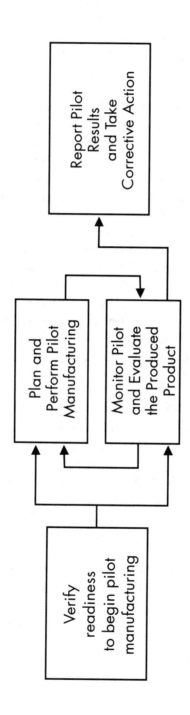

Figure 10.3. Pilot manufacturing activities.

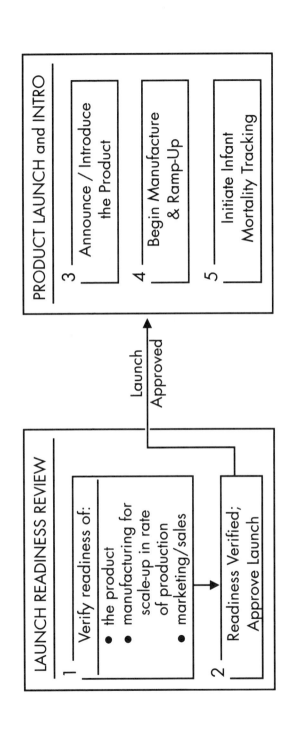

Figure 10.4. Readiness for product launch.

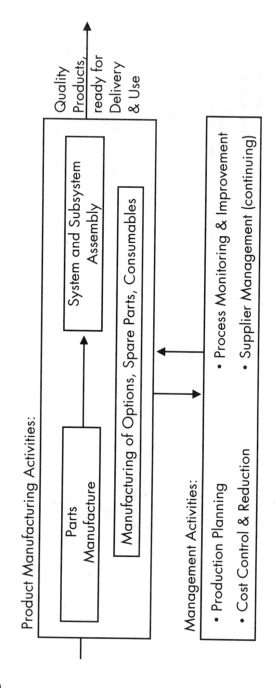

Figure 10.5. Volume manufacturing activities.

these firms during the 1980s were primarily aimed at regaining some level of parts quality, which had declined steadily as the number of parts suppliers proliferated. The minimization of suppliers mentioned in chapter 9 is in large part a reaction to this supplier proliferation and the resulting loss of control of parts quality.

Essential Elements

The essential elements for superior product manufacturing enable a product development project to be planned and executed with the appropriate emphasis on the quality of the manufacturing and delivery processes. They form a basis for integrating parts manufacturing and system assembly operations into one functioning whole. They ensure that the critical variables of the product are controlled properly during the manufacturing process. They can be divided into the essential elements for parts manufacture and the essential elements for system assembly.

The essential elements for parts manufacture are:

- The team controls the suppliers;
- The number of suppliers is minimized;
- Process control is implemented at the point of manufacture;
- All parts manufacturing processes are certified as capable; and
- Inventory is kept to a minimum.

The essential elements for system assembly are:

- The team controls the first six months of production;
- Critical manufacturing is performed in-house;
- Replication capabilities are demonstrated;
- Processes are verified;
- Stress tests of critical variables are conducted;
- The "simplify first, automate last" concept is implemented. and;
- an infant mortality program is initiated.

A method for formalizing the transfer of critical product information to the manufacturing process is presented. Appropriate implementation of these essential elements is imperative if superior results are to be achieved and the major manufacturing quality problems which occurred throughout many US industries during the 1970s and 80s are to be avoided.

A Single Product Development and Manufacturing Team

Although the single product development and manufacturing concept was discussed in chapter 2, it merits repeating here, as it continues to be the single most influential element affecting the entire product development process, including this phase. The most successful teams in our case studies were generally responsible for everything from technology selection to manufacturing and delivery, for up to six months after the product's introduction.

Elements Affecting Parts Manufacture

Control of the parts manufacturing process in the case studies was critical to achieving product quality objectives. Thus, parts acquisition and control were not blindly delegated to other organizations. Essential elements affecting parts manufacture are discussed below.

Team Responsible for Supplier Selection and Coordination. In most of the studied cases, supplier selection was controlled completely by the development-manufacturing team and not by an independent functional organization. This approach required a change in management practices so that the team controlled the organization's procurement practices instead of a materials management or procurement organization. Supplier decisions were based on ensuring a continuous flow of quality parts and assemblies with a minimum of scrap, rework, and service costs.

In a few cases, the overall functional management structure was unchanged, but a procurement member was assigned to, and located with, the development-manufacturing team. When the procurement organization was used, it understood that the development team was to select and control suppliers, not the bidding process. Development team managers in the case studies considered supplier selection based on capability – not the lowest bid – as an extremely important element in the project's success. During company personnel interviews, no other subject invoked such intense feelings as did the control of supplier parts. Virtually every group previously had experienced serious quality problems based on parts obtained via the low-bid process.

Minimization of the Number of Suppliers. All of the companies studied have strived to reduce parts quality problems by minimizing the number of suppliers and by establishing certification programs for their parts manufacturing processes. They have reversed the "supplier roulette" process that maximized bidding, increased the number of suppliers, and created major quality and cost problems.

One major firm uses single sourcing with early supplier identification to control the manufacturing process. Single sourcing is used exclusively, unless domestic-content laws require that a percentage of the product be manufactured in the same country in which the product is sold. This single source strategy enabled the company to reduce its forward product supplier base from 5,000 firms to 300 firms [Bebb, 1989].

Process Control at Point of Manufacture. Volumes have been written about statistical process control (SPC) techniques to control manufacturing processes, so these methods will not be discussed here except to mention that they must be used effectively and not just for show. The effective use of SPC requires that it be used at the point of manufacture by production personnel to stop the creation of bad parts at their sources. Therefore, the essential element of process control is the statement, "at the point of manufacture."

Process Certification. Process control at the point of manufacture was equally important for supplier-produced parts. The selected single-source suppliers were required to certify process control for each part number by sending the process control information with every parts shipment. These suppliers were not blanket certified, but instead were certified on a part shipment basis. Suppliers became partners in the manufacturing process and were rewarded with long-term contracts for their efforts. This long-term, contractual partnership provided an incentive for continual parts quality improvement, which reduced long-term parts costs by reducing scrap and rework [McLeod, 1989].

Minimum Inventory. The companies we studied understand the Japanese axiom "inventory is the enemy" and are acting to reduce it. Eliminating multiple suppliers, lowering parts inventory, and reducing bidding require significant organizational changes and thus encounter considerable resistance. The materials management and procurement bureaucracies are so entrenched in many US firms that it is difficult to implement the necessary changes.

For example, the MIT working group study [Dertouzos et al., 1989] found serious competitive problems throughout the US auto industry regarding the procurement of parts from suppliers as compared to Japanese practices. The American focus on short-term supplier contracts and frequent switching to cheaper suppliers greatly impeded communication between key parts makers and vehicle managers. The MIT group concluded that US firms must decrease emphasis on "legalistic, adversarial contractual agreements," and instead promote long-term relationships, as Japanese firms do. The parts procurement bureaucracy is illustrated graphically by the numbers the group presents: GM employs 6,000 buyers versus Toyota's 337, and an average GM plant needs 1,500 first-tier supplier firms compared to Toyota's 177.

The firms in the case studies were overcoming these barriers and were improving their manufacturing processes by making these changes during the early 1980s. The US automobile industry, led initially by Ford and Saturn and now by Chrysler, is finally making the significant changes needed to become competitive.

Elements Affecting Product Assembly

Several of the essential elements apply particularly to the firm's product assembly processes. The financial impact that assembly processes exert on the product depends upon the type of product and how it was designed. For some products that have been designed to be simple to assemble, assembly costs may account for less than 5 percent of the product's overall cost [Janssen, 1987; Galatha, 1988; and others]. But for other products, such as automobiles, final assembly accounts for about 15 percent of the total manufacturing costs [Womack et al., 1990, p.58]. In either case, assembly processes can critically affect the quality of the final product.

Product Team Responsible for the First Six Months of Product Manufacture. Under the single team, the development and manufacturing team is responsible not only for the product design but also for pilot product manufacture. (Of course, the team is provided with additional resources to enable pilot manufacture to be conducted.) The team's responsibilities end not at the traditional "release to manufacture" checkpoint used in functional organizations but at a "proof of manufacture" point that occurs about six months after the start of production. The team's manufacturing responsibilities are defined at the beginning of the project, when the team is formed.

In the case studies, we found the team approach to manufacturing to be quite different than that for a functional structure. The ultimate objective within the product teams is to complete manufacturing successfully, including the timely delivery of the product to the customer. Thus, the team's project goals are all geared to successful product manufacture rather than just to a release to manufacture. When the team's product designers share responsibility for successful product manufacture, the design emphasis changes from "getting the design finished so that we can give it to manufacturing" to "completing the design that can be manufactured with the highest quality and lowest cost."

Critical Manufacturing and Assembly Processes Performed In-House. In many of the case studies, the parts and assemblies critical to the product are specially designed and manufactured to give the product a distinct competitive advantage. These advantages are achieved by advancing the state of the art for important product features and their associated manufacturing processes.

In most of these cases, the manufacturing process advances are developed in-house and kept proprietary to preserve competitive advantage and to maintain maximum quality control and improvement. In other cases, very close partnerships with specialty suppliers are established to achieve the advance.

For example, a pen plotter development team formed a partnership with an innovative plastic molder and die maker to develop advanced molding techniques for their disposable plotter pens. The new techniques enabled the pen parts to be made to extremely small tolerances, which allowed fast, automated pen assembly and improved pen performance. Based on this experience, the firm now has designated single sources for all of its plastic parts from one of three designated molding suppliers. When a new project team is formed, die maker and molding firms are selected to work with the team and its parts designers throughout the entire project [McLeod et al., 1989].

The proprietary hot roll for a copier was manufactured in-house to ensure control of critical material, thickness, and other parameters of the part [Wilson, 1979]. One printer team developed proprietary, in-house processes to ensure that all print quality standards would be met during product manufacture.

Replication Capability Demonstrated (by Pilot Run and Test) Prior to the Start of Full-Scale Manufacturing. Manufacturing processes developed in the studied cases were tested thoroughly to ensure that they were capable of replicating the new product assembly. The teams conducted full-scale tests to ensure that their processes were capable of making defect-free products in the production environment. Some companies used the terms "pilot run" or "manufacturing verification test" to describe this activity. Controlled increases in production volumes were used to verify production capability in an orderly manner. One firm not only requires a manufacturing scale-up to full production, but also mandates customer testing of pilot-run produced products before the product can be introduced to the general market [Xerox, 1988].

Manufacturing Processes Verified. The importance of using characterized, verified processes to manufacture world-class products was summarized well by members of a color inkjet printer team:

> Use standard, well-understood processes. Historically, when we have strayed from this concept we have suffered low yields, cost increases, and many engineer hours of process support and characterization. [Smith et al., 1988]

In the case studies, the primary manufacturing goal was to ensure the quality and reliability of their processes. Development teams met this need by limiting manufacturing processes to those that were well understood and characterized. These characterized processes, then, were verified as being capable of meeting the product engineering specifications.

Process verification obviously is dependent on the quality of the process design. For one advanced manufacturing firm, process verification begins in the Manufacturing System Design phase of product development. Their manufacturing system design plan includes several key requirements. First, each process must be verifiable; that is, methods must exist to ascertain that "you did it right." Next, no "black art" processes are permitted; that is, all key performance attributes must have quantifiable failure rates. Also, processes must be "engineering-free"; that is, processes must function without ongoing support from engineering.

Critical Variables Stress Tested. A most difficult assessment for some products is to determine whether the assembly process has adversely affected the reliability of critical product functions. Short-duration functional check tests demonstrate only one-time, nominal operation and provide no indication of the function's reliability (unless its reliability is so poor that it fails the functional tests). Without a manufacturing reliability assessment, products that pass factory functional tests may be shipped to customers, only to fail as soon as the product experiences a slight variation in operating conditions. To address this problem, manufacturing stress testing was used in selected cases to verify that the functional operating space of the product was not compromised during product assembly.

For example, high-speed copy machines are stress tested to ensure document handling reliability after initial system assembly. A paper stress pak, consisting of many different paper thicknesses and types, is used to test the document handler's ability to process the wide variety of papers that might be used in the copier. Because the document handler's operating space includes all of the stress pak paper types and thicknesses, *any* manufacturing test failures indicate an incorrect assembly or a faulty part and thus signal the need for corrective action. No copier is permitted to be shipped without passing this test as error-free. The use of this "stress screen" preserves the design reliability of the document-handling function through the assembly process.

A manager of a popular automated tape cartridge drive system attributes "the early improvement in the drive . . . to the early implementation of stress screening." However, management support and rapid corrective action were required for successful implementation, since stress screening substantially affected initial production yields as latent defects were uncovered [Abbott, 1989].

The need for management support and rapid corrective action during the implementation of stress screening must not be underestimated. The use of a manufacturing procedure that deliberately imposes production limitations (i.e., stress testing and its resulting product failures) may be considered an "unnatural act" to a manufacturing organization that normally is measured by production quantities. A potential conflict is created when factory production volume is deliberately sacrificed to prevent a potential customer failure. The management of the production measurement system must prioritize the elimination of field failures over the volume shipment of supposedly "good" products that actually have latent defects.

A stress screening strategy is affected greatly by technology, materials, and design decisions, and thus has to be formulated specifically for each product. To be effective, the stress test needs to attack important product failure modes and must test the product at a sufficient stimulus level while the product is operating. Provision must be made for product failure diagnosis and repair [Burcak, 1986]. Although stress testing is controversial and must be managed properly to be effective, it is important enough that one major firm in 1983 established a worldwide corporate strategy to incorporate systematic stress testing during product design and manufacturing [Hayes and Wheelwright, 1984].

The "Simplify First, Automate Last" Concept Implemented. The "simplify first, automate last" concept is implemented. Several teams developed their product and manufacturing systems concurrently. Products in several of the case studies were designed for automated robotic assembly. Product assembly time and complexity were reduced dramatically by minimizing the number of parts and by using snap-together techniques in the product's design.

In these cases, the need for robotic assembly was brought into question after the design was completed, since human assembly of the simplified design was trivial and virtually error-free. In one case where robots already had been purchased and installed, robotic assembly methods were implemented as planned. However, when product assembly later was transferred to another manufacturing location, the robots were left behind and human assembly used instead, except for a few select operations. The change was made because robot setup and maintenance costs were excessive when compared to simple human assembly. The lesson learned is this: *simplify the product design as if a robot were going to assemble it; then carefully choose what operations are worth the investment of robotic assembly* [Janssen, 1988].

Infant Mortality Corrective Action Program Implemented. Nothing may surprise product engineers more than to see the product fail as they follow it into the customer environment. (In many firms, engineers are never provided this opportunity and must depend upon the service organization to inform them of problems.) For new platform products (i.e., first-generation products) particularly, there is a need to have an infant mortality program that is *dramatically more responsive than the typical warranty program* normally conducted by the regular service, manufacturing, and engineering departments. IBM conducted a successful infant mortality program with its large Model 60 copier to ensure that it would not have the problems that plagued its predecessors. The Saturn Corporation eliminated a potentially serious customer engine problem by recalling and replacing more than 500 new automobiles found to contain defective antifreeze that might have damaged those engines. This well-publicized recall immediately established Saturn as a "different kind of car company" to all customers who have experienced warranty problems with other firms. An infant mortality program, discussed below, is an essential element of a successful new product development.

Infant Mortality Monitoring Program

The successful introduction of a new platform product, such as a new, first-generation automobile, copier, printer, computer, or medical instrument, often depends on its early reputation for reliability and dependability. There are a few well-publicized stories of major field failures of products, but multitudes of instances that are not well known. Of course, it is in a firm's best interest to recover from their product failures as quickly as possible and not to broadcast them. Product developers need to know that if they do not manage their efforts properly to minimize customer-experienced failures they run the risks of embarrassing publicity and expenses large enough to destroy their firm financially. Therefore, the challenge for new product introductions is to *avoid failures by taking very careful preventive measures.*

This book has illustrated how to avoid such failures from the initial idea throughout the entire product development process, but the last chance for major prevention comes at the new product launch time. The last preventive essential element is the establishment of an infant mortality corrective action program. During initial product launch, the sources of product failure are often very different from each other, which causes them to be classified as the one-of-a-kind failures often associated with parts or assembly quality problems. The term "one-of-a-kind" translates into "no engineering action," since changing the design of parts is reserved for failures that significantly affect the field population.

A typical reaction in functional organizations is for quality/manufacturing engineering to classify most product problems as engineering or service problems, engineering to classify these same problems as mostly manufacturing or service problems, and service to classify them as manufacturing or engineering problems. The result is an immediate three-way gridlock. With today's customer demands for near zero field failures, *every* field failure must be investigated by a team that includes engineering, manufacturing engineering, and service skills, so that enough information to ascertain the root causes of the failures can be obtained. This team needs to be directed by management to solve problems by removing them from the product and the customer, and to not spend time assigning blame and cost responsibility.

The following is an outline of an infant mortality corrective action program that worked very well during the market introduction of a new high speed copier. Another firm followed a similar approach when introducing their new forklift truck with very good results. The guidelines for establishing a product infant mortality assessment program are:

- Establish a field performance control group (FPCG) within the product development team;
- Require product field service personnel to report *all* product failures and customer comments to FPCG by telephone or facsimile for a limited period of time after product introduction (perhaps about 90 days);
- Require that all failed parts/modules/product be returned to the FPCG for failure analysis and perform failure analysis on every returned item;

- Set up a customer hotline and ask customers to report all product problems, questions, and failures;
- Track the failure and service history of specific machines and follow these machines into the field and record all failures, maintenance actions, and problems that occur;
- Have FPCG personnel visit the tracked machines regularly to evaluate their performance by examining the historical record and by performing specific stress tests on the product;
- Establish a Field Problem List that defines the observed problem, the root cause of the problem, the corrective action, the person responsible for ensuring that the corrective action is completed, and target completion dates (the FPCG directs any additional action that is necessary);
- Track the product's actual failure rate versus the predicted reliability for the product and take corrective action until the actual reliability reaches the goal; and
- Require appropriate engineering, manufacturing, and service persons (whether or not they are product team members) to report to FPCG about field problems on a weekly basis to ensure timely action.

An FPCG is established as a mini-team within the overall product development team dedicated to ensuring that the product meets the goals set for reliable performance in the customer's environment. Information gathering is immediate with the use of facsimile machine feedback on all product failures. The facsimile machine is a definite improvement over verbal telephone reports, which could lead to error and lack of structure because they have to be transcribed. A customer hotline provides an important parallel input that cannot be modified by either the firm's service or marketing personnel.

The return of all failed parts has a very significant effect in bringing failure information quickly back to the team. This practice quickly allows for the identification of the difference between failed parts, improperly manufactured parts, or improper service diagnosis. The tracked service history is particularly valuable for separating inadequate engineering or manufacturing from inadequate service. FPCG personnel visit customers, thus providing the additional benefit of instilling a sense of urgency for eliminating failures that cannot be matched from within the firm.

The Field Problem List is a critical document that reveals weaknesses in product performance, shows the corrective action plan, and assigns responsibility for implementing corrective action. The FPCG has responsibility to direct additional action if it deems current actions to be inadequate. Tracking the actual failure rate versus the predicted rate enables the team to determine whether corrective actions are improving the product quickly enough to meet the product's reliability goals. Corrective action may have to be accelerated if goals are not met as projected. Finally, the FPCG communicates directly with top management to ensure that the corrective action plans are executed properly.

The quick gathering of information by a group dedicated to identifying and solving problems through rapid remedial action makes the difference. Having this infant mortality action plan as a designated part of the product launch enables unexpected problems to be caught and managed early enough to eliminate some major customer exposure to problems. With the problems managed to ensure the product goals of reliability and high quality, the product development team can turn the product over to the manufacturing function in an orderly fashion, usually with the manufacturing members of the team transferring to the manufacturing functions. The rest of the team then can be "cycled back" to begin the development of more new products.

Summary

The measurable results of this phase are the execution of the planned launch of the product to the customer and the pleased reaction of the customer to the product. The final report of the Field Performance Control Group on the product performance and the customer satisfaction with the product is a critical document that must be examined. Customer acceptance is measured by examining the actual demand for the product versus the projected demand forecast by the marketing and business targets. Marketing and service execution versus plan is also evaluated. Only if all goals are met satisfactorily has the product development team completed its work.

The amount of manufacturing support training needed is reduced dramatically from traditional release-to-manufacturing transfers because the product development team is responsible for manufacture through the first six months of production and key members of the team transfer to the manufacturing organization. Of course, engineering drawings, specifications, and other documentation – particularly the specially identified critical dimensions and process specifications – are transferred. Manufacturing System Design phase information describing the current manufacturing system and plans is also transferred. At the six-month evaluation point, the next year's actions are planned, as the product is transferred from the product development team to the manufacturing, marketing, and service organizations to continue the firm's support of the new product.

References

Abbott, Tom (1989), Storage Technology Corporation, correspondence dated August 30, 1989.

Bebb, Barry (1989), "Quality Design Engineering, the Missing Link in U.S. Competitiveness," paper presented at National Science Foundation Design Theory Workshop, University of Massachusetts, June 1989.

Burcak, T. (1986), "Application of Stress Screening To Commercial Products," *Proceedings of the Institute of Environmental Sciences*, pp. 317 – 320.

Dertouzos, Michael L., Richard K. Lester, Robert M. Solow, and the MIT Commission on Industrial Productivity (1989), *Made in America – Regaining the Productive Edge*, MIT Press, Cambridge, MA.

Galatha, Matthew (1988), "Design for Automation – The IBM Proprinter," notes from a lecture at the University of Tennessee, Knoxville, TN, April 14, 1988.

Hayes, Robert H., and Steven C. Wheelwright (1984), *Restoring Our Competitive Edge: Competing Through Manufacturing*, New York: John Wiley and Sons, 1984.

Janssen, D. (1988), "A Diskette Drive Design for Automatic Assembly," course notes from ASME short course, "Case Studies of Engineering and Manufacturing Methods for Superior Results," Atlanta, GA, April 18 – 19, 1988.

McLeod, G., et al. (1989), interviews with members of the Hewlett-Packard Plotter Pen and Paintjet teams, San Diego, CA, May 1989.

Smith, J. C., et al. (1988), "Development of a Color Graphics Printer," *Hewlett-Packard Journal*, Palo Alto, CA, August 1988, pp. 16 – 20.

Wilson, Clement C. (1979), "A New Fuser Technology for Electro-photographic Printing Machines," *Journal of Applied Photographic Engineering*, Summer 1979, pp. 148 – 156.

Womack, James P., Daniel T. Jones, and Daniel Roos (1990), *The Machine That Changed the World*, Rawson Associates, New York.

Xerox Corporation (1988), "Product Delivery Process Overview (PDP)," Business Products and Systems Group, Webster, NY.

CHAPTER 11

LEADING AND ORGANIZING PRODUCT DEVELOPMENT

Management and Organizational Effects

Changing Management and Organizational Practices

Management and organizational practices today are in an unprecedented state of flux. Organizations everywhere are "re-engineering," "flattening," "leaning," "downsizing," "restructuring," "buying out," "partnering," trying to become "customer driven," and so forth. Employees are being "empowered," "released," "retired but hired back as temporaries," "self-directed," "broadened," "cross-trained," and so on. The new graduate professional enters this environment hoping to make substantial contributions to the improvement of US competitiveness and trying to start a career of some substance. If these new graduates are somewhat confused, there probably is good reason.

Resistance to Change

A model of competitive practices like the one presented in this book is certainly beneficial for understanding the product development process and the essential elements of superior product development. However, within every organization there are different degrees of freedom with respect to how the product development process may be constructed. Organizations that have strong, bureaucratic, functional organizations (like engineering, marketing, manufacturing, purchasing, service, and product test) may strongly resist the use of the single-team product development model. This resistance is basically one of control; the single-team approach used in the product development process means that the team leader has control over the team and resources related to the project. If the team leader has this control, then functional managers do not.

Even when functions appear to support the integrated product team concept, functional managers often will hedge by only loaning their personnel to the team. Often these loaned members still have responsibilities in their functional group and their performance is still appraised by the functional manager. Finally, these loaned members may be substituted by other persons if priorities change in the functional department. Obviously, these practices weaken the team and results even though the approach gives the appearance of an integrated product team.

Traditional use of metrics and rules to assess the performance of employees and the firm may also run counter to superior product development practices. Innovative new products "destroy" capital in the sense that they make previous product generations obsolete and force the firm to upgrade or replace the capital equipment used to make those products. Metrics that motivate production workers to run their machines as much as possible to attain the highest machine utilization generate piles of excess inventory along with all the other problems that go with that practice. Metrics used to smooth the workload in a purchasing department, such as giving buyers up to 45 days to issue requests for bids, frustrate the project manager, who is trying to develop an innovative product on a challenging schedule.

Succeeding in Spite of the Organization

Some highly motivated teams do succeed, in spite of the firm's organization, by figuring out how to work around these organizational barriers. In many cases, team leaders successfully negotiate a hands-off policy so that the team can meet an aggressive development schedule. A classic example is the IBM personal computer team, which was permitted to bypass IBM's marketing, procurement, real estate and construction, manufacturing, and other functional groups. Furthermore, IBM PC team members were issued restricted phone numbers to prevent divisional IBM staff organizations from contacting them. By isolating the PC team from these "regular" organizations, the personal computer was developed on an 18-month schedule.

Some US Firm Results

Many once-dominant US firms like IBM, Chrysler, Dupont, Kodak, General Motors, Alcoa, Westinghouse, and Xerox fell on hard times throughout the 1980s. Xerox appears to have corrected its competitiveness problems early enough to recover. Chrysler was once dangerously troubled, but has rebounded significantly with the introduction of their LH product line and other "cab-forward" designs. These new, competitive products, now recognized as superior, have resulted from a new product development structure, including use of an integrated product team and many of the other ideas that are discussed in this book.

In the mid-1980s, Ford recognized its need for improvement much more quickly than did General Motors and introduced the very successful Taurus family of automobiles (using the single-team "TeamTaurus" organization). General Motors responded by creating the Saturn Corporation and found that the team-based approaches arising from "a different kind of company" were able to create a car that was rated above all other GM cars in customer satisfaction, and bested only by the Lexus and the Infiniti, two Japanese luxury cars [J.D. Powers Customer Satisfaction Survey, 1994]. Based on these positive results, GM is now attempting to "Saturnize" some of its other divisions to improve their product development capabilities.

The Requirement for Competitiveness

To be competitive in the 1990s and beyond, a firm's organizational management will have to become compatible with superior product development practices. Development dysfunction resulting from functional extremes cannot be tolerated, because competitors are implementing organizational structures and practices that are not only compatible with but directly support superior product development practices. Additionally, the best firms encourage continual improvement in their product development processes. Firms that waste their energies fighting internal conflicts simply will not survive; constantly improving competitors will pass them by.

The leadership needed to reverse the counterproductive practices in many firms is substantial. The challenge for these managers is to understand much more than the bottom line. They

229

must understand the complete product development process and how to improve its effectiveness on a continual basis. In short, they must construct their organizations to be creators of superior products that not only meet but anticipate the needs of their customers. These organizations must be able to modify their practices as they learn the art, skill, and methods of developing superior products and processes. We believe that this book can provide a head start for those who want to improve the way their firm develops new products.

Project Management Using the Product Development Model

Recognize That Each Project Is Different

The key to using the Product Development Process Model successfully is to realize that each project is indeed different. The product development process is used to build the roadmap for that project to follow. The resulting activity for any specific project may be dramatically different, depending upon whether the new product is a derivative product, a new platform product, or a breakthrough product requiring the development of new technologies.

Plan for the Differences Using the Model

Team leaders can review each phase to see what is required to meet the milestone goals for that phase. If product and manufacturing technologies that have already been developed are to be used in a derivative product, the Technology Selection and Development phases can be quite short and may require only some technology feasibility statements to clarify their status. If common modules can be used in 70 percent of a new product, the Design and Evaluation phase can focus on the newly designed 30 percent and the system evaluation. However, if new configurations, features, or benefits will be necessary to meet customer needs, the Product Ideas and Customer Future Needs phases will need enough emphasis to enable the development of a new product description. The development process model helps the team by encouraging a comprehensive look at the total process so that an effective product development project plan can be synthesized. Information outputs at the end of each phase and at scheduled reviews encourage the proper scorekeeping *by the team* on the progress of their project.

Recognize the Need for Effective Team Integration

The integration of persons from functions critical to successful product development (including hardware and software engineering, manufacturing, and marketing) into an effective team is the most fundamental requirement for success. Technical skills must match the technical task to be done. With highly skilled people in each area, the team can function effectively with the least number of people. Obviously, selecting an effective leader is also critical to the success of the project.

Manage the Teamwork

Effective teamwork is not an accident; nor does it come automatically. Management of the team is a major (and continuing) task. Communications must occur so that all team members share the same vision for the new product and become motivated toward its success. Evaluation methods used to assess the performance of team members must not divide the team or demoralize them; for this reason, team-based success measures are increasingly used. Leaders (managerial, technical, or otherwise) must act like coaches for the whole project and not be divisive. The team leader must create an environment where team members feel free to talk about *all* problems that potentially endanger the project's success and to take actions to assure success. The term "ownership of the problems by the team" really does have meaning to those who have had the good fortune to be part of a successful, integrated team. Team members that feel this ownership assume responsibility for problems and solve them, rather than expecting someone else to solve them or blaming others.

The relationship between ownership and problem solving is important because the standard operating mode of those in traditional functional organizations has been to blame other groups for their problems. Team members coming from these organizations may bring that history and their bad habits with them. The team's leaders must recognize this situation when it occurs and take action to correct it immediately.

Keep Score and Adapt

Product development efforts inevitably experience surprises along the way, no matter how simple the project. The surprises may arise from technical, marketing, or manufacturing sources. One subsystem in a product may unexpectedly generate electrical emissions that confound information being received from a microprocessor in another area. The firm that the team expected to use as its major market channel may back out at the last minute and have to be replaced. A major competitor may announce a product with a new feature. A new part may be much more difficult to manufacture than expected.

To minimize the number of surprises, superior teams keep score on their product's performance, their project's performance, and their manufacturing process performance. *Nonetheless, there will still be surprises.* Teams that keep good scores on themselves, their product, and their process get earlier and clearer warnings of impending problems than those who do not. Thus, they can solve or adapt to them sooner and at less difficulty and expense. Good teamwork management and problem ownership by the team enable problems to be discussed and solved without having to lay blame. In this positive environment, the team's major challenge is to find an acceptable solution to the problem quickly. Often, friendly competition may arise in seeing who can solve the problem first − a far cry from the delaying tactics and finger-pointing which often occurs in contentious functional organizations. Glenn Gardner, the team leader for the Chrysler cab-forward automobiles, has said that the integrated product team used to develop those vehicles enabled product development to move faster and with fewer problems than he had ever experienced.

Product Development Improvement – The Lexmark International Example

Lexmark International is a former division of IBM, based in Lexington, Kentucky. When purchased in a leveraged buyout around 1990 by Clayton Dubilier, the division was primarily a supplier of small printers and computer keyboards. The site had had a long history of successful product development, beginning in the 1960s when it was the electric typewriter division, IBM's smallest division. In the 1970s, the Lexington facility became IBM's largest division (the office products division) by developing a large number of successful products, including the Selectric typewriter, electronic typewriters, dictation equipment, the Displaywriter word processor, copiers, and high-speed laser, inkjet, and impact printers. At the time of the buyout, however, the site was perceived, like much of IBM, as suffering from unaffordable and bureaucratic business methods.

As Lexmark, the firm began searching for methods that would enable them to compete head-on with Japanese printer competitors. One of their most impressive achievements from this effort thus far has been the development of the only US-made personal laser printer, which is marketed by IBM as the IBM 4019 laser printer. (The engines for Hewlett-Packard's laser printers are made by Japan's Canon Corporation.)

In conjunction with their pursuit of even more effective product development methods, Lexmark then developed their next-generation printer, the IBM Model 4037. The objectives for this printer development project were to create a high-quality laser printer, to reduce cost significantly, and to demonstrate a much improved product delivery (i.e., development) process. The figures and the brief discussion that follow illustrate both their success and a major cause for that success – the use of a concurrent engineering approach similar to that presented throughout this book.

Figure 11.1 illustrates the overall product delivery process used to create the 4037 printer. Clearly the process synthesized

Product Delivery Process

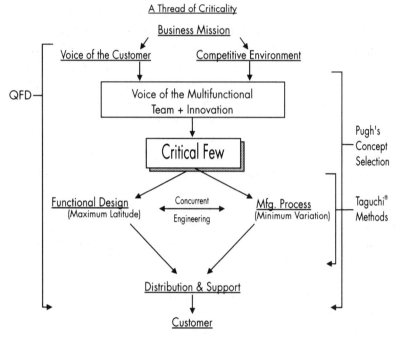

Figure 11.1. Illustration of the Lexmark product development process for the IBM 4037 laser printer (courtesy of Lexmark International.)

Lexmark's business mission, which had to respond to both the voice of the customer and a very competitive environment. The voice of the customer and the competitive environment fed into the voice of the multifunctional team, within which *innovation* was a critical ingredient. The customer voice was interpreted via the effective use of quality function deployment (QFD) techniques, which involved the direct interaction of customers with the development team. Pugh's concept selection methods were used to choose and develop the product's configuration (as discussed earlier in chapter 7). Their approach emphasized a *thread of criticality* throughout the process. In every phase, the *critical few* items were focused upon as a matter of their process i.e. the *critical few* technologies, product features, business items, manufacturing processes, distribution methods, service methods, etc. Their concept of concurrent engineering focused on functional design for maximum latitude (i.e., the widest possible operating space for product functions) and on developing appropriate manufacturing processes that have minimum variation. As shown, Taguchi® methods were used to support these activities.

At the beginning of the project, the potential time savings resulting from using the concurrent engineering approach (as opposed to the traditional linear model) was projected (see figure 11.2) and used to justify the effort. One can note the significant increase in the relative up-front, concept design work that was projected before the team was to begin detailed design work. By spending more time at the concept level, Lexmark estimated that it could reduce the number of revisions and iterations to achieve a 40-percent reduction in the project schedule.

Figure 11.3 shows the actual performance of the 4037 printer development team – a 22-percent total time savings versus the previously developed 4019 printer. The team's perfor-mance confirms that the major benefits result from the reduction in revisions and iterations. As part of a total comparison, it is important to note that although the 4037 was a new platform product it is still in some ways a derivative of the 4019, in that the 4037 team was able to at least study and perhaps use parts of the 4019 configuration.

Other improvements resulting from the improved process used to develop the 4037 are summarized in the following list. The number of people needed was reduced by an impressive 67 percent, an achievement even if one thinks of the 4037 as a derivative of the previous product. Improvement in the 4037 product's reliability is no less impressive, as demonstrated by the elimination of emergency engineering changes and an 80-percent reduction in warranty costs. One benefit not noted in the list is that the print quality of the 4037 scores much better in tests than did the previous product.

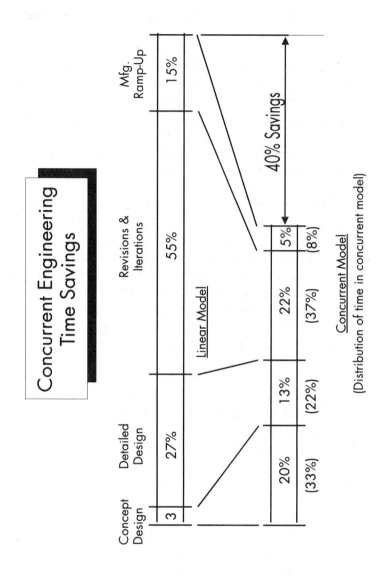

Figure 11.2. Start-of-project estimates of time savings (and task distribution over time) for developing the Lexmark 4037 laser printer using concurrent engineering (courtesy Lexmark International).

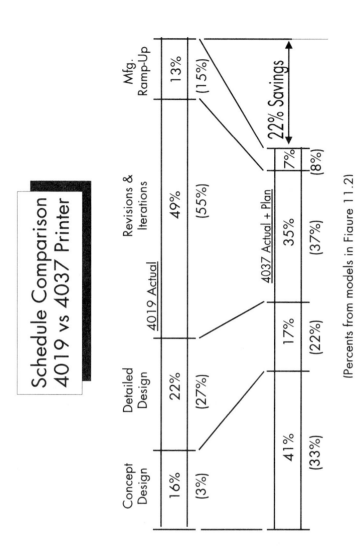

Figure 11.3. The actual time savings (and task distribution over time) achieved during the development of the Lexmark 4037 laser printer through the use of concurrent engineering techniques (courtesy of Lexmark International).

- Delivered in record time
  - 33 vs 37 months from scratch to announce
  - 23 vs 34 months from critical staffing to announce
- $\frac{1}{3}$ the number of people
- Less than $\frac{1}{2}$ had previous product delivery experience
- World-class plastics development & tooling process developed
  - $\frac{1}{2}$ time for design & tooling
  - High quality first time tooling cycle
- Zero emergency Engineering Changes, no major field concerns
  - 1 to 8 on previous releases
- First product to start production w/parts on Pull
- 80% reduction in warranty cost
- Aggressive cartridge stability targets achieved in 25% planned time

Finally, the following list illustrates the results achieved by the development team from their use of Dr. W. Edward Deming's "plan-do-check-act" cycle. Forty-one product development techniques and strategies were studied to compare the 4037's team performance with Lexmark's business-as-usual efforts. The results (both good and bad) presented in the list clearly indicate that the development team has made an honest, if not critical, self-assessment. However, the team recognized that *complete honesty during the self-assessment is needed if the team is to improve its performance on the next project.*

41 Elements studied
- Worse than business as usual
  - Staffing
  - Cost management
  - Leadership
  - Marketing plan
  - Models
  - Follow-on plans
  - Recognition
  - Use of contractors

- Better than business as usual
  - Use of field and customer data
  - Concept selection
  - Design for ease of use
  - Teams
  - Early manufacturing involvement
  - Vendor partnerships
  - Use of extended team
  - Engineering release process

Epilogue

The Lexmark example illustrates the tremendous effort needed to use, and the rewards that can be gained from, an improved product development process. It is difficult to develop a new product development process at the same time as the new product, but today's – and tomorrow's – competitive environment demands it. We believe that the Lexmark example illustrates well many of the key principles that are presented in this book. Special thanks go to Mr. Greg Survant, Lexmark project team leader, for sharing the Lexmark 4037 development team's experiences in a Superior Engineering Design Program Seminar at the University of Tennessee during the spring semester of 1994.

References

J.D. Powers Customer Satisfaction Survey, 1994.

Selected Bibliography

Peace, Glen Stuart (1993), *Taguchi Methods®: A Hands-On Approach*, Addison-Wesley, Reading, MA.

Pugh, Stuart (1991), *Total Design: Integrated Methods For Successful Product Engineering*, Wokingham, England: Addison-Wesley.

DISCUSSION QUESTIONS

These discussion questions have been provided to help course instructors and students use the book in classroom settings. They can be used to trigger class discussions or can be given as assignments.

Chapter 3: Product Ideas

1. Divide the class into teams of three or four people. Determine at least five product concept ideas.
2. Following the process in figure 3.2, screen your ideas and develop a product concept description for your best idea. State all the assumptions that you are making about your firm and its constraints.
3. Present your product idea in a 3-minute presentation to the class.

Chapter 4: Customer Future Needs Projection

1. Compare the features of three different telephone answering machines. Identify the one that you feel is the benchmark for quality and functions.
2. Define a product that you know about and project at least one future need. Defend this need by discussing how the customer will use the product function that meets this need.
3. Define at least two critical quality characteristics of the product considered in the previous question.
4. How would you propose measuring these quality characteristics?

Chapter 5: Technology Selection and Development

Consider a product that you have previously designed or examined.

1. What were the critical variables?
2. How would you go about characterizing the operating space?

Chapter 6: Final Product Definition and Project Targets

Divide into small teams to discuss the following questions.

1. Develop a final product definition for a product. What are the critical questions that you must ask to develop the final product definition?
2. Generate a timeline for development of this product and place appropriate project milestones on it.
3. Develop product descriptions of the base product and two derivative products.
4. Develop a proposed business plan with the key items that must be considered.

Chapter 7: Product Design and Evaluation

1. Create a product design specification for a product that you previously selected.
2. Identify the modules and/or subsystems of this same product.
3. Create a comprehensive test plan for this product.
4. Describe the difference between testing for failure and testing for success. Identify each in your comprehensive test plan.
5. Which parts of this product should be tested as parts or modules?

INDEX